SHUTTING OUT THE SKY

SHUTTING
LIFE IN THE TENEMENTS OF NEW YORK 1880-1924
OUT THE SKY

DEBORAH HOPKINSON

ORCHARD BOOKS / NEW YORK
AN IMPRINT OF SCHOLASTIC INC.

For

Elisa Johnston,

a girl from Jones Street

LIBRARY OF CONGRESS CATALOGING-IN-PUBLICATION DATA
Hopkinson, Deborah. Shutting out the sky : life in the tenements of New York, 1880–1915 / by Deborah Hopkinson.— 1st ed. p. cm. Summary: Photographs and text document the experiences of five individuals who came to live in the Lower East Side of New York City as children or young adults from Belarus, Italy, Lithuania, and Romania at the turn of the twentieth century. Includes bibliographical references. Contents: Coming to the golden land — Tenements: shutting out the sky — Settling in: greenhorns and boarders — Everyone worked on — On the streets: pushcarts, pickles and play — A new language, a new life — Looking to the future: will it ever be different?
ISBN 0-439-37590-8
1. Urban poor — New York (State) — New York — Juvenile literature. 2. Immigrants — New York (State) — New York — History — Juvenile literature. 3. Tenement houses — New York (State) — New York — Juvenile literature. 4. New York (N.Y.) — Social conditions — Juvenile literature. [1. Poor — New York (State) — New York. 2. Immigrants — New York (State) — New York — History. 3. Tenement Houses. 4. New York (N.Y.) — Social conditions. 5. New York (N.Y.) — History — 1865–1898. 6. New York (N.Y.) — History — 1898–1951.] I. Title.
HV4046.N6H66 2003   307.76'4'097471 — dc21   2002044781

1 2 3 4 5 6 7 8 9 10   07 06 05 04 03

Printed in the U.S.A. 24 › First edition, October 2003 › Book design by David Caplan
The display type was set in Trajan and Liberty BT. The text type was set in 12-pt. Granjon.

TABLE OF CONTENTS

FOREWORD

*I*N OLD PHOTOGRAPHS OF NEW YORK CITY'S TENEMENTS, WE SEE STREETS AND MARKETPLACES OVERFLOWING WITH CROWDS OF NAMELESS IMMIGRANTS. Before 1880, more than 5 million people, mostly from Ireland, Germany, and other places in western Europe, came to America. The failure of the Irish potato crop and famine from 1845 to 1850 drove about 2 million Irish people to emigrate. In Germany, crop failures and poor economic conditions also forced many to leave their homes.

But these numbers were small compared with the tidal wave of immigrants that flooded America's shores in, approximately, a forty-year period at the turn of the nineteenth century. Between 1880 and 1919, historians estimate that about 23 million people came to America with about 17 million entering through the port of New York. The majority of these immigrants came from eastern and southern Europe, including Russia, Poland, Romania, Hungary, Czechoslovakia, Lithuania, Italy, and Greece. Immigrants also arrived from many other areas, including Finland, Germany, Britain, France, Norway, Denmark, Sweden, and Syria.

Shutting Out the Sky covers these years of peak immigration, from 1880 until 1924, when the Johnson-Reed Act, also called the Immigration Act of 1924, established the first permanent limitation on immigration. The Immigration Act of 1924 limited immigration to about 165,000 people annually, established a quota system based on country of origin, and barred Japanese immigrants.

With such vast numbers of people, it is sometimes hard to remember that each was an individual, with his or her own family, culture, and dreams. This book introduces immigrant life in New York City at this time through the voices and stories of a just a few of the young people who journeyed to this country as immigrants, and made America their home.

VOICES IN THIS BOOK

 *Rose Gollup Cohen* was born Rahel Gollup in Belarus in 1880. She came to America in 1891 or 1892 at the age of twelve.

Leonard Covello came from Avigliano, Italy. He was born in 1887 and came to America in 1896 at the age of nine.

 *Maurice Hindus* hailed from the village of Bolshoye Bykovo in Belarus. Born in 1891, he came to New York in 1905.

Pauline Newman's exact birth date is unknown. But we do know she was born in Lithuania around 1888 and came to America in 1901.

 *Marcus Eli Ravage* was born in 1884 and immigrated to America from Romania in 1900, at the age of sixteen.

COMING TO THE GOLDEN LAND

The gold you will find in America will not be in the streets. . . . It will be in the dreams you realize — in the golden dreams of the future.
— LEONARD COVELLO, *Italian immigrant,*
recalling his grandmother's parting words

✣ WATCH FOR THE BUTTERFLY ✣

In a small mountain town in southern Italy, young Leonard Covello waited by the window. Even when the wind blew hot and humid, he stood looking westward, past the cobbled streets, the piazza, and the ancient stone walls of his town.

Life was hard in Avigliano, where Leonard was born. Harvests were often poor. Water was scarce. Each day Leonard's mother caught rainwater in tubs for washing and went to the town well to fetch drinking water.

Leonard's father had tried several trades, including shoe making. But it became too hard to eke out a living in Avigliano. When Leonard was about three, his father left for America to find work. In America, people said, it was possible to make your fortune.

Leonard, his mother, and two younger brothers stayed behind, living in one room in his uncle's house. One of Leonard's earliest memories was helping his mother write letters to his father. Like most girls in the village, his mother had never been to school, and she could neither read nor write.

Leonard missed his father, and often waited by the window until his mother called him away.

"You must watch for the butterfly," Leonard's mother said, trying to comfort him. "When a butterfly enters the window, then we will have news of your father, and it will be news that he is sending for us."

Sometimes Leonard caught butterflies and turned them loose inside the house. But it didn't work. His father still did not return.

ꞙ STORIES OF THE GOLDEN LAND ꞙ

Some people said about America: "All you have to do is to get a big shovel and a sack, and you go into the street and shovel the gold into the sack."

— ABRAHAM GAMBERG, *Ukrainian immigrant*

Marcus Eli Ravage was a boy in Vaslui, a small town in Romania, when he first heard stories about America. In America, it was said, a man could earn enough in one day to buy yards and yards of calico, two sacks of rye, and a whole tub of butter.

Not only that, soap was so cheap, even the poorest people could wash with it. Not just once a week, but every day! Women no longer would have to wash linens with yellow sand scooped out of the bottom of the river.

Peasant women in Russia

When a man from Vaslui who had gone to New York returned for a visit, the entire town buzzed with excitement. The visitor wore a top hat and a fancy coat, and even a diamond ring. Surely, Marcus thought, this man was a millionaire. Marcus was convinced that if he could only get to America, he, too, would soon be rich.

In the middle and late 1800s, stories about America spread rapidly in small Jewish towns in Russia and eastern Europe. People often gathered in the marketplace to listen to a letter read aloud in Yiddish from a cousin or brother who had gone ahead. Sometimes the letter even contained gold pieces. Real gold, all the way from America!

Struggling families listened eagerly to stories about a place where you could have water flowing out of a faucet, right in your own house. A place where anyone could buy meat — all you wanted, and cheap. A place where everyone could afford to drink tea with lots of sugar in it. A place where even a poor boy could become a doctor or a millionaire.

It's no surprise they wanted to hear more about a place called "the golden land." It's no surprise they wanted to go to America.

WHY DID THEY COME?

Immigrants came to America for different reasons. For Italian families like the Covellos, America offered a chance to escape grinding poverty.

In Italy, poor families like Leonard Covello's didn't have their own land, but worked as laborers for others. Toward the end of the nineteenth century, even farmers who did own land were struggling, due to poor economic conditions and changing world markets for goods. Unemployment rose as successful orchards in Florida and California hurt orange and lemon growers in Italy, and high French tariffs disrupted Italy's wine industry.

In Romania, young Marcus Ravage was convinced that emigration was his only chance to escape the poverty of his town, and to get an education. Laws in Romania discriminating against Jews made it almost impossible for him to go to a university or start a successful business.

For eastern European Jewish families like the Ravages, America offered the promise not only of gold, but freedom from religious persecution. For hundreds of years Jewish people had lived in an area of eastern Europe under the rule of the Russian Empire called the Pale of Settlement. This region included Poland, Belorussia, Ukraine, and Lithuania.

Eastern European Jews shared a common religion, culture, and language: Yiddish. Most lived in a Jewish town, called a shtetl, which contained wooden houses, shops, and a central marketplace where people brought livestock and vegetables to sell.

The restrictions against Jews led to great poverty. Russian immigrant Morris Raphael Cohen remembered how hard Jewish housewives in his town worked, chopping wood, baking bread, and drawing water from the well. The women had to wash their families' clothes in the river, almost a mile away. In winter, when the river froze, they cut holes in the ice. On wash days the women shuffled carefully over the icy ground carrying their wash, a washboard, and a wooden mallet to pound water from the clothes. It was a heavy load to carry home.

The Jews of eastern Europe had often been subject to unfair rules and repression because of their religion. In 1882, Russia's May Laws placed

Washing laundry on an ice-covered lake

further restrictions on Jews. They weren't permitted to own or rent land outside towns and cities. Students were forced out of schools and colleges. The government's pressure on Jewish people didn't stop there. Pogroms, or massacres of innocent Jewish people, began to take place more frequently. As fear spread among the Jewish community, emigration often seemed the only hope for the future.

Ukrainian immigrant Abraham Gamberg remembered, "I was only eight or nine years old when we had a pogrom in our city. Mobs of Russians, non-Jewish people, robbed our stores; some Jewish people were killed. I hid in the cellar with my brother for three days without food. I couldn't see that we had done anything wrong to anybody — why should we be persecuted?"

Although they came from different places, spoke different languages, and practiced different religions, Jewish and Italian immigrants would soon find themselves neighbors, working and living side by side — along with immigrants from many other places — in some of the most densely crowded neighborhoods in the world.

⤳ SAYING GOOD-BYE ⤝

So at last I was going to America! Really, really going, at last! The boundaries burst. The arch of heavens soared. A million suns shone out from every star. The winds rushed in from outer space, roaring in my ears, "America! America!"
— *MARY ANTIN, Russian immigrant*

Many families who wanted to come to America couldn't afford to make the voyage together. Often the father would travel first to find work and save the "passage money" to bring the rest of the family over. In 1896, after six years in America, Leonard Covello's father was finally able to send for his family. It was time for nine-year-old Leonard to say good-bye to his grandmother, Mamma Clementine, who was in her nineties. Leonard tiptoed into her room, breathing in the familiar scents of lavender and olive oil. Then he leaned close to kiss her.

Leonard understood he would never see Mamma Clementine again. Perhaps that's why he always remembered the words she whispered in his ear. The gold he would find in America would not be in the streets, Mamma Clementine told him, but in the dreams he would realize — the golden dreams of the future.

Marcus Eli Ravage was sixteen in 1900, the year he convinced his parents to sell the family cow to pay for his journey from Romania to the United States. His mother packed jars with jam and pickles for him to eat. She knitted socks and mended his shirts, and tried to persuade him to take his old overcoat with him. Marcus refused. In America, he felt sure, he would soon be rich enough to buy a new coat.

On the day Marcus left, his mother seemed calm. But as the train drew into the station, she began to cry. She clung to Marcus desperately, as though her heart would break. At the time, young Marcus could not understand her despair.

"I understand it now," he wrote many years later. "I never saw her again."

Preparation for the trip often took months as families made clothing, stocked up on food, and packed belongings. The family sometimes had to travel far by train or river just to reach a port city where they could board a ship for America.

A family leaving for America was a special event, something to remember for years to come. To Maurice Hindus, who left his Russian village in 1905, it seemed as though everyone in the village turned out to say good-bye, forming a long, noisy procession. Women cried and waved; neighbors hugged the travelers and shouted last-minute advice.

Although leaving home could be hard, for some young people the journey to America was an exciting adventure. Immigrant Mary Antin could hardly sleep during her last night at home in her Russian town. "In the morning I was going away . . . forever and ever. I was going on a wonderful journey. I was going to America. How could I sleep?"

The next day, as the train chugged away, she turned back for one last look. Then "the station became invisible, and the shining tracks spun out from sky to sky. I was in the middle of the great, great world, and the longest road was mine."

"...home was something from which one never parted, even as the tree never parts from the earth. . . . Now there was to be a complete break . . . the native earth would chain me no more."
— *MAURICE HINDUS, Belorussian immigrant*

✒ THE JOURNEY ✑

My heart leaped up at the beautiful sight. I had never seen a real ship before. Here was the gate of the great world opening up before me, with its long open roads radiating in all directions.

— *MARCUS ELI RAVAGE, Romanian immigrant*

"On the fourth day a terrible storm came," said an Italian immigrant named Rosa Cavalleri, recalling her voyage from Italy in 1884. "The sky grew black and the ocean came over the deck . . . Us poor people had to go below. . . . We had no light and no air and everyone got sick . . . We were like rats trapped in a hole, holding onto the posts and onto the iron frames to keep from rolling around."

Most immigrants traveled across the Atlantic as third-class passengers in steerage, below the deck of the steamship. People were crowded together in horrible conditions, without water or toilets. The stench was almost unbearable, as most immigrants suffered from seasickness during the voyage, which typically took two to three weeks.

Pauline Newman was a young girl when she made the journey to America from Lithuania in 1901 with her widowed mother and two sisters. She never forgot her crossing. "It was horrible. We were down in steerage, and the food was mud puddles . . . unless you had tea of your own, you wouldn't get any tea, you'd get boiling water. . . ."

Pauline never forgot the kindness of one sailor who brought her an orange and carried her up on deck for some fresh air. "Another time he brought me two sardines on a roll," Pauline recalled many years later. "He must have known that the food was rotten and he was very nice."

Pauline's trip was made even worse by the fact that her family's luggage became lost. All their family treasures — everything they had brought with them — were gone, including all the records of the children's birth dates. Pauline grew up never knowing exactly how old she was.

*The Statue of Liberty and
New York Harbor*

THE GREAT BARTHOLDI STATUE.
LIBERTY ENLIGHTENING THE WORLD.
THE GIFT OF FRANCE TO THE AMERICAN PEOPLE.

Then one day we could see land! Me and my paesani *stood and watched the hills and the land come nearer. Other poor people, dressed in their best clothes and loaded down with bundles, crowded around. America! The country where everyone could find work! Where wages were so high no one had to go hungry! Where all men were free and equal and where even the poor could own land! But now we were so near it seemed too much to believe. Everyone stood silent — like in prayer. Big sea gulls landed on the deck and screamed and flew away.*

— ROSA CAVALLERI, *Italian immigrant*

Leonard Covello and his two little brothers hadn't minded the trip across the ocean. For his mother, it was different. When storms and angry waves had tossed the old ship up and down, she had clutched her children close to her heart in silent terror, too frightened even to cry out.

It was natural for Leonard Covello's mother to be afraid. After all, she'd never ventured more than a few miles from her small mountain town. Now she had entered a frightening, unknown world. She had taken her three young boys on a train to Naples, and kept them safe for twenty days on a crowded boat across the stormy Atlantic.

When Leonard's family arrived in New York, they went directly from the boat to the immigrant processing center, where immigrants were given eye and physical examinations. Men, women, and children entering the country through New York passed through Castle Garden, or, when it opened in 1892, through Ellis Island.

Leonard remembered how frightened his mother was of losing her children in the crowds and confusion. His mother barely closed her eyes. "Once during a physical examination men and boys were separated for a short time from the women. My mother was frantic as the guard led me and my two younger brothers away. When we ran back to her, she clutched us . . . in her eyes there was the disbelieving look of a mother who never expected to see her children again."

Immigrants at Ellis Island

$\mathcal{R}$ose Cohen was born on April 4, 1880. When she was twelve, Rose and her aunt Masha made the long journey to America from their Russian town. Her father was already working in New York City, saving money to bring the rest of the family to America.

Once they had finished their physical exams and were free to go, Rose and Aunt Masha peered through the crowd watching for Rose's father, who was supposed to meet them. Rose was almost afraid she wouldn't recognize him. After all, it had been more than a year since she had seen him.

Italian immigrant family

Rose scanned the crowd anxiously. Where was he? Finally, Rose spotted a man smiling and waving at them. Her father at last!

In the midst of her joy, Rose stared at her father in confusion. Back home he had worn a full beard and long earlocks, the custom for Orthodox Jewish men. But now that he lived in America he had shaved his earlocks and trimmed his beard. Rose could hardly believe how different he looked.

As millions of young people like Rose were to discover, just about everything in America would be different.

Immigrant children at Ellis Island

Long before Europeans came, Native Americans lived in the area we now call the state of New York. One group of Native Americans, speaking the Algonquian family of languages, included the Lenni Lenape (Delaware), the Shinnecock, and the Mahican peoples. The other group, who spoke languages in the Iroquois family, included the Mohawk, Oneida, Seneca, Cayuga, and Onondaga.

In September 1609, a Dutch ship called the *Half Moon* entered a large, deep harbor (the New York Harbor of today). Its captain, an Englishman named Henry Hudson, had been hired by the Dutch East India Company to search for a trade route to Asia. Hudson saw a large island with two rivers on each side of it. This was the island the Lenape Indians called "Mannahata" (Manhattan), which is usually translated as "hilly island."

By 1626, the Dutch West Indies Company had founded several small trading posts in the region as well as a permanent settlement, New Amsterdam, on the lower tip of Manhattan Island. That same year the Dutch bought Manhattan from the Native Americans for sixty florins' worth of goods. The colony stayed under Dutch control until 1664, when the English took over and renamed the colony New York. New Amsterdam got a new name, too: New York City.

New York City's location at the mouth of the Hudson River made it well suited for business and trade. By 1743, it was the third largest city in the American colonies, and by 1760, only Philadelphia was larger. In

1790, New York City's population included more than 28,000 whites, about 1,000 free blacks, and about 2,000 slaves. Slavery was not officially abolished in New York until the 1820s.

During the 1800s, industrialization in America exploded. By the middle and late 1800s, New York was a major center for banking, printing, exports and imports, and manufacturing. In 1898, New York City was expanded to include not only Manhattan, but four other boroughs — the Bronx, Brooklyn, Queens, and Staten Island — making New York City the largest city in the nation as well as its leading port.

Tenements: Shutting out the Sky

I shall never forget how depressed my heart became as I trudged through those littered streets, with the rows of pushcarts lining the sidewalks and the centers of the thoroughfares, the ill-smelling merchandise, and the deafening noise . . . So this was America, I kept thinking . . . the opportunity to live in those monstrous, dirty caves that shut out the sunshine.

— Marcus Eli Ravage

✐ FIRST IMPRESSIONS ✐

As the ferry pulled away from Ellis Island toward Manhattan, Leonard Covello looked up shyly at the man beside him. His father seemed so much taller and stronger than he remembered. Then Leonard noticed his father's thick, dark mustache. That, at least, was just the same.

Leonard's father and mother stood at the ferry railing, happy to be together again. It had taken six years, but Leonard's father had at last earned the passage money to reunite his family. Now he was eager to show them America.

Immigrants like Leonard carried bundles of clothes, household

Immigrants take their luggage from Ellis Island

goods, and a few precious family treasures. They also brought hopes, dreams, and expectations. Would America be anything like the world they'd imagined for so long?

As he looked around, young Leonard couldn't help feeling overwhelmed at first. "The cobbled streets. The traffic of wagons and carts and carriages and the clopping of horses' hoofs . . . The endless, monotonous rows of tenement buildings that shut out the sky . . . Dank hallways. Long flights of wooden stairs and the toilet in the hall. It was, he wrote later, as if all the warm sunlight and fresh air of his mountain home in Italy had been replaced by four walls and people on every side.

Rose Cohen was bewildered at her first sight of New York, too. Her father had hired a wagon to bring Rose and Aunt Masha to his tenement apartment on the Lower East Side. As Rose bumped along the cobblestone streets tucked into the wagon among their bundles, she couldn't help but feel a rush of emotions.

"My thoughts were chasing each other," she recalled. "I felt a thrill:

'Am I really in America at last?' But the next moment . . . I felt a little disappointed, a little homesick."

You couldn't get to love a tenement flat; it was not home. We never stayed long in one flat anyway. That was the way it was in the big city. People moved from house to house, from one neighborhood to another, never missing the old place, glad perhaps never to have to see it again.

— *MAURICE HINDUS*

Immigrant family in tenement apartment

Immigrants brought with them a strong sense of family, clan, and community. They wanted to live close to where they could find jobs, and to be near relatives and friends from back home. As more immigrant families arrived, certain parts of New York became very crowded. Most crowded of all was the lower, eastern part of Manhattan, an area called the Lower East Side.

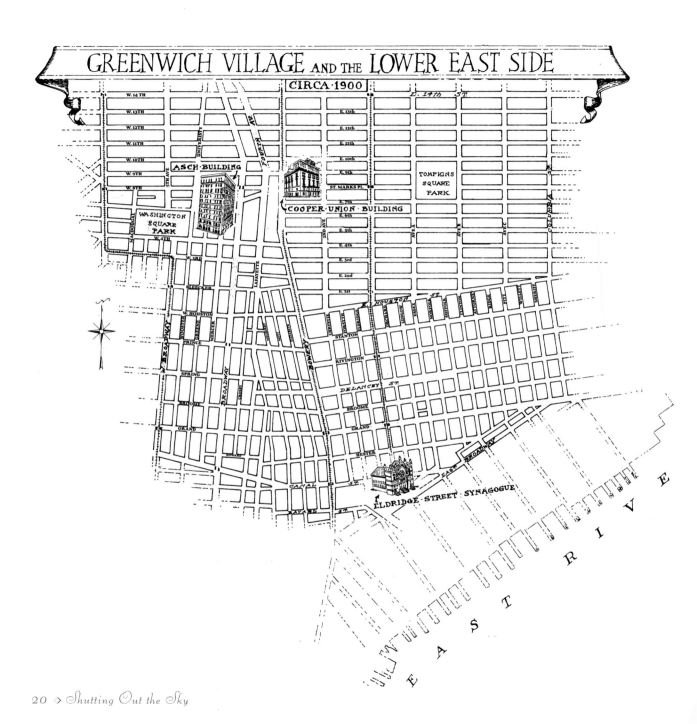

GREENWICH VILLAGE AND THE LOWER EAST SIDE

CIRCA·1900

Although neighborhood divisions have changed slightly over time, traditionally the Lower East Side was bordered by Fourteenth Street on the north, on the west by Broadway and Pearl, on the east by the East River, and on the south by Fulton Street. Within this area, immigrants clustered together, often living near one another on the same streets to create distinct sections such as Little Italy, Chinatown, or Little Romania.

Alleyway behind tenements with outhouses

In the early and mid-1800s, immigrants from Holland, Germany, Poland, and Ireland settled in this area, drawn by shipyard and construction work, and the many small shops and factories that offered unskilled jobs. Although some Chinese immigrants lived on the Lower East Side, their numbers did not grow as rapidly as other groups because of laws in the 1870s and 1880s that restricted immigration from China. Chinese people weren't allowed to come to the United States, and those who were in America were not permitted to become citizens or own property.

Around 1845, a wave of Irish immigrants arrived, pushing out earlier residents of the Lower East Side. Many free black families who had lived on the Lower East Side relocated to Greenwich Village, in an area near Washington Square that became known as "Little Africa." (Following the Civil War, many Southern blacks moved to New York, and by 1910 the city had more than 90,000 African-American residents, compared with 20,000 in 1860.)

When immigrants from Russia and Italy began to pour into the city during the latter part of the nineteenth century, they, too, were drawn to the Lower East Side. The number of Italians in New York City grew from 44,230 in 1880 to 1,343,125 in 1910, as the city became home to more Italians than anywhere else in North America. About 2 million eastern European Jews immigrated to the United States from 1881 to 1914. By 1910, there were about 1.4 million Jews in New York City, with more than half a million on the Lower East Side.

It's no wonder the Lower East Side began to burst at the seams with people. By 1890 there were about 520 people per acre on the Lower East Side. By 1900 there were more than 700 people per acre.

⤷ WHERE WILL THEY LIVE? ⤶

"In the stifling July nights…, men and women lie in restless, sweltering rows, panting for air and sleep."
— *JACOB RIIS, Danish immigrant and reformer*

As immigrants flowed into New York City, builders rushed to construct housing quickly and cheaply. The most cost-effective way to meet the demand for housing was to put many families in the same building. These multifamily apartment buildings were called tenement houses. The law defined a tenement as any house occupied by three or more families living independently and doing their own cooking on the premises.

To make more money, builders and landlords tried to fit as many people as possible into their tenements. They often subdivided rooms and constructed tenements with narrower hallways. Builders constructed tenements closer together, too. Once the buildings were done, most landlords never bothered to make improvements. After all, there was no shortage of

Italian family's tenement apartment

tenants. In addition to the Lower East Side, tenement districts grew up in other parts of New York, including East Harlem (where Leonard Covello and his family lived) and Brownsville.

Big Flat was a huge, six-story brick tenement built in 1855. It took up six lots between Elizabeth and Mott streets on the Lower East Side, making it the largest building of its kind in New York before the 1880s. Big Flat started out as model housing, but conditions deteriorated over time. Few improvements or repairs were ever made. By the time it was torn down around 1889, Big Flat had become known as one of the worst tenements on the Lower East Side.

Big Flat's tenants lived in dark, airless rooms. There were piles of garbage in the hallways. Because the sinks leaked, many of the walls and floors were wet and smelly. The toilets on the upper floors didn't work well, and

A rear tenement

the health department eventually closed them. That meant all five hundred tenants had to use twenty-eight toilets on the first two floors.

Other tenement buildings had no toilets inside at all. Around 1907, Pauline Newman lived with her family in a tenement on Madison Street. It was, she said, "a tenement without facilities . . . no bathing facilities, no bathroom, no toilet; the toilet was in the yard. And that was the same in the next tenement, and the next."

The blocks of tenement buildings were crammed ever more tightly together. And although some laws regulating standards for tenements were passed in the 1860s and 1870s, they weren't always enforced.

By the middle of the 1800s, reformers, housing activists, and tenant groups in New York had begun to call for improved conditions. Some new buildings with "model tenement" designs began to appear. The reformers also passed codes to improve sanitation, overcrowding, and fire safety.

Many of these early efforts to provide decent housing failed. The regulations were weak and difficult to enforce, and landlords were not willing to give up their profits. Sometimes middle-class reformers blamed the immigrants and tenants themselves for their poverty and poor housing conditions.

But efforts for reform continued, and in 1890 a call to action came from a journalist who was an immigrant himself: Jacob Riis.

⊰◐ HOW THE OTHER HALF LIVES ◑⊱

It is said that nowhere in the world are so many people crowded together on a square mile as here.

— *JACOB RIIS*

Jacob Riis

𝒥acob Riis was born on May 3, 1849, in Denmark, and came to New York in 1870. He struggled to find work, and sometimes found himself without a place to live. But Riis was bright and determined. Eventually he became a newspaper reporter for the *New York Tribune,* covering the police beat and working out of an office on the Lower East Side.

As Riis roamed the back alleys and streets he was appalled at the horrible living conditions. He decided to do something about it. The invention of flash photography enabled him to take photos at night and inside buildings. In 1890, Jacob Riis wrote a book, *How the Other Half Lives,* with such powerful pictures and words that readers were carried directly into the world of the tenements.

"Suppose we look into one?" he suggested. ". . . Be a little careful, please! The hall is dark and you might stumble over the children pitching pennies back there . . ."

Riis took his camera everywhere. His photos showed children and parents crowded in small, dim rooms. He also called attention to rear tenements, which were built close behind other buildings. He took

Mulberry Bend

pictures in the narrow alleyways between two tenements, showing just how crowded and dark they were.

"The rays of the sun, rising, setting or at high noon" never touch buildings such as these, Jacob Riis wrote. The only part of the heavens people who lived there could see, he told his readers, was a "strip of smoke-colored sky."

⚬ REFORMS ⚬

What are you going to do about it? is the question of today.

— *JACOB RIIS*

How the Other Half Lives shocked its readers. The book was an immediate success, and a renewed call to action for social reformers. Even today, it is considered one of the most influential books ever written in America.

Throughout his life, Jacob Riis continued to write and speak out about poverty and housing reform. One of the areas he called attention to was a crime-ridden part of Mulberry Street called "the Bend." In 1897, this area was razed and made into a park. When the park was dedicated, the crowd gave Jacob Riis three cheers.

Gradually, partly as a result of the work of Jacob Riis and other reformers, housing reforms began to take place. The Tenement House Law of 1901 emphasized better lighting, sanitation, and new fire and safety standards. New tenement buildings could be only six stories high. Owners were required to provide fireproof shafts and stairwells, and one toilet for every two apartments. Also, buildings were only allowed to cover 70 percent of a 25-by-100-square-foot lot, eliminating dark inner courtyards and increasing the size of backyards.

The new law required landlords to install cold water faucets inside each apartment instead of only providing cast-iron sinks in the hallway or backyard. It also created a Tenement House Department. The first head of the department, Lawrence Veiller, tried to force builders to meet the law.

One builder in 1906 remarked that before the Tenement House Department was established, "you weren't bothered while putting up your building and when it was finished it was finished and in went your tenants. Now you can't begin to think about tenants until the Department hands over your certificate."

Also, in the early 1900s, immigrants became more active in fighting for their rights. In 1902, alarmed at the cost of kosher meat rising from twelve to eighteen cents a pound, immigrant housewives and working women organized a meat boycott and forced sellers to lower prices. When in 1904 many landlords began increasing rents, women organized again. Tenants held rent strikes and blocked evictions.

Immigrant Pauline Newman led a rent strike in her Madison Street tenement building in 1907, when she was about nineteen years old. When the landlord asked for a rent increase, she organized the tenants, who told the landlord they would pay the higher rent if he would put a toilet in the hall. Pauline recalled that the landlord wouldn't do it, so the tenants didn't pay an increase.

". . . the families did not have a private toilet, but had to use one in common with others in the tenement, sometimes as many as four families using the one toilet, often filthy, dark and with plumbing out of order."
— LOUISE ODENCRANTZ, *social worker and writer*

Yet despite these efforts, many immigrants still lived in poor housing, and many "old-law" buildings remained. In a study of families living in New York published in 1907, social worker Louise Bolard More found four common types of apartments. The worst were very old rear houses, or rear tenements. In these houses, she reported, halls were dark, stairs rickety, and floors almost worn through.

In another type of older tenement house, only the front rooms had windows to the outside, and the kitchen and bedrooms had windows looking into a public hall or into an air shaft. These tenements usually

House behind tenements

had four apartments on each floor, each of which rented for ten to fifteen dollars a month.

A better class of old tenements had two apartments on each floor, each consisting of four or five rooms and renting from fifteen to twenty-five dollars a month. Finally, there were the best and most expensive apartments in "new-law" tenement houses. These boasted more outside windows and five or six rooms in each apartment. But they also cost more. Families paid eighteen to thirty-two dollars a month for such apartments.

Despite the conditions in many tenement buildings and the demands on their time, immigrant women worked hard to create a home and to make their apartments clean and attractive.

In most tenements, colorful curtains hung at the windows, bright carpets covered the floors, lace doilies adorned simple shelves and bureaus, and religious pictures or family portraits decorated the walls. In her book published in 1907, Louise More wrote of an immigrant mother who saved a few cents each week in order to buy some lace curtains as a surprise for her children.

The kitchen table was usually covered with oilcloth to make it easier to clean. And some families put plants or window boxes in the windows to make their homes more cheerful.

A NEW HOME

When Leonard Covello's mother arrived in the fall of 1896, she knew nothing about tenement laws or housing reform. But she did know that everything around her seemed new and strange.

The Covellos lived near other immigrants from their town in southern Italy. One neighbor, Carmen Accurso, arranged a welcoming party for the newcomers. Leonard's mother sat dazed, unable to take it all in.

Mrs. Accurso put her arm around Leonard's mother and led her into the hallway to show her something extraordinary: a sink and water faucet right inside the house. Leonard recalled how she encouraged his mother, saying, "Courage! You will get used to it here. See! Isn't it wonderful how the water comes out?"

For the first time in days, Leonard's mother smiled.

Once Rose Cohen had arrived safely at her father's small apartment on the Lower East Side, she felt too timid to go beyond the front steps of her tenement. Nothing looked familiar to Rose. "I saw many streets, rows and rows of brick houses, crowds of people . . . With a sick feeling of fear I shrank back into the hall."

But soon Rose would step outside, into her new world. She would become part of the noisy tenements, streets, and neighborhoods of New York.

Settling In: Boarders and Greenhorns

Life here is not all that it appears to a greenhorn . . . Here you will have to pay for everything . . . the rent, for the light, for every potato, every grain of barley.
— Rose Cohen

∽ RICH, OR POOR? ∾

One early morning in December 1900, a sixteen-year-old boy left Ellis Island and made his way alone into New York City. Struggling with his heavy bundles, Marcus Ravage elbowed his way through the crowded streets of the Lower East Side.

Marcus shivered in the bitter cold. If only he'd followed his mother's advice and brought his heavy coat to America. He'd been so sure he wouldn't need it. After all, he'd argued, why should he bother carrying old clothes when he'd soon be rich enough to buy new ones!

But Marcus had brought something almost as precious as a warm coat, and with cold fingers he dug into his bundles to find it. It was just a crumpled bit of paper, but it was a link between his old life in Romania and his new one. On the paper was scribbled the New York address of distant relatives from back home.

Before long, Marcus found himself in the apartment of the Segal family, who had arrived from Romania just three months before. Mrs. Segal, along with her son and five daughters, lived in a five-room apartment on the third floor of a Rivington Street tenement. Looking around at the sofa, kitchen table, and ever so many chairs, Marcus felt sure that the Segals were already rich. And he wouldn't be far behind.

Mrs. Segal told Marcus he could stay for free for a few days. After that, he would be expected to find a job and pay fifty cents a week for his bed. With seven members of the Segal family plus him, the apartment would be crowded, Marcus thought, but it was better than being out on the street.

A tenement apartment

That evening, people Marcus had never seen before began to stream into the apartment, tired from a long day of work. *Who were all these strangers?* Marcus thought. As the hours ticked by and the strangers didn't leave, Marcus realized they were boarders — they lived there, too! They paid Mrs. Segal for a bed, and perhaps for meals and laundry. *Where would everyone sleep?* he wondered.

Marcus soon found out. It wasn't long before everyone began to rush about, lining up chairs in rows to make beds. Marcus and three other young men shared the sofa, sleeping with their heads on the cushions and feet propped awkwardly on chairs. Nine bodies pressed together on the floor, huddling like seals on a rock. In the kitchen, Mrs. Segal and one child cuddled on top of the washtubs while the rest of the children slept on the floor. And the room Marcus thought was the children's bedroom? A family of five had taken it over.

Soon the rooms were filled with deep breathing, dreadful snoring, and smells of all kinds. Yet despite his new, strange circumstances, Marcus fell asleep right away. Next morning he woke to the puffing of steam engines and clatter of wheels outside the windows. Once again the rooms hummed with activity. People raced to put the furniture back into place; the men scrambled to get dressed before the girls awoke. Mrs. Segal crammed extra feather beds into nooks and crannies and made coffee.

After everyone else had hurried off to work or school, Marcus and Mrs. Segal were left alone in the now neat and tidy apartment. Since Marcus was still considered a guest, Mrs. Segal wouldn't hear of him helping with the housework or marketing. He was thoroughly surprised to see Mrs. Segal clean the kitchen floor with precious soap rather than sand, as his mother would have back home.

When Mrs. Segal came back from the market,

"We had to keep our windows closed because the cinders from the train would come in the house.... It was so hot in the summer, you couldn't breathe. We slept on the fire escape or in the yard where the toilets were."
— *ROBERT LESLIE, physician and printer*

Marcus felt more confused than ever. She'd bought the largest eggplant (which some immigrants called a "blue tomato") he'd ever seen, as well as an exotic yellow fruit in the shape of a cucumber — a banana. And then there was a cauliflower, a vegetable his father had eaten only once in a big city and had talked about ever since. To say nothing of meat — which she cooked for lunch!

Back home in his village only rich people could indulge in the luxury of meat in the middle of the day, eat such extraordinary vegetables, use soap instead of sand to clean floors, or live on the second floor of such a nice apartment.

But, Marcus puzzled, if the Segals were rich, if they had *already* made their million dollars in three months, why did they share their fine apartment with so many boarders?

To a newcomer, or "greenhorn," like Marcus, it was all very confusing.

✦ BOARDERS AND LODGERS ✦

When Rose Cohen stepped out of the wagon and into the tenement building where her father lived, she found that, like the people sleeping in the Segals' apartment, her father rented space in someone else's house.

Rose's father paid for the use of a single room from the Felesberg family — a husband, wife, and three children. The tiny, cramped quarters would have to do for Rose and her aunt, too. Rose didn't mind so much. After all, she had come with a goal: to earn money to bring her mother and younger brothers and sisters to America.

Mrs. Felesberg told Rose her husband earned twelve dollars a week pressing coats. To Rose, that seemed like a lot of money. But Mrs. Felesberg explained that back home they'd had their own small house and garden for food. Here in New York City, everything had to be paid for. If the Felesbergs didn't rent out a room, they wouldn't be able to make ends meet.

Many immigrant families took in boarders or lodgers. At Mrs. Segal's house, breakfast was included in the rent. The people who stayed there were called boarders. Those like Rose and her father, who cooked their own meals, were usually referred to as lodgers.

Boarders or lodgers were often relatives or neighbors from the same village back home. Taking in individuals was more common among Jewish families than Italian ones. Sometimes, though, two Italian families would share an apartment, dividing the space so each family could eat and sleep separately. These "partner households" helped keep the rent low, which was important to immigrants relying on low-paying, irregular jobs.

Taking in boarders and lodgers led to overcrowded living conditions in the tenements. Yet many immigrant families could not survive without the extra income. In 1908, one expert estimated that about one out of every four immigrant families had a boarder.

❧ MOVING ❧

We liked moving from one place to another. Everyone on Cherry, Monroe and other streets moved often . . . moving even from one dingy place to another is a change. And . . . some were less dingy than others. Here, for instance, the living room, instead of being painted an ugly green that had made everything look dark, and that had depressed our spirits, was a bright pink.

— ROSE COHEN

Another way families coped with high rents and low incomes was to move often. Eddie Cantor, who grew up with his immigrant grandmother on the Lower East Side, remembered moving if they couldn't pay their rent on time, or when the landlord discovered that instead of two people in the apartment, ten or twelve were living there.

Moving was easy to do, Eddie recalled. The main cost was hiring a pushcart. "This my grandmother loaded herself with a chest of drawers, a half-dozen mattresses, an iron bedstead, a few stools, some kitchen utensils . . ."

Then, with young Eddie perched on top of the load, off they would go to yet another new home.

GREENHORNS: NEW CUSTOMS

For the first few days, Rose Cohen felt so terrified by the noise and rushing crowds, she didn't venture any farther than the tenement stoop. Her father and aunt left early for work, and Rose was often lonely and homesick. Huddled in the doorway, she watched hundreds of people hurry by without seeing a single face she knew.

One day Rose wandered to the roof of the tenement. The roof was flat, and she could see other roofs stretching out in all

Italian man with baby

Tenement laundry lines   directions. Some had clotheslines on them, with freshly washed shirts and pants fluttering in the breeze.

But what Rose noticed most was the sky. Just looking at it filled her with joy, as though she had suddenly found someone dear from home. She said to herself, "The sky is the same everywhere. There is only one. Perhaps Mother, too, Sister or someone at home is looking at it this very moment."

When Rose did begin to venture out, she started to realize how America was changing her father. On Rose's first Saturday, her father invited her to choose a piece of fruit to eat from a peddler's cart in the street. In her town back home, a Jewish person would not handle coins on the Sabbath. Rose assumed her father had credit with the peddler and would pay later for the fruit, as he would have done at home.

As she was about to take a bite of melon, Rose spotted the glint of a coin in her father's hand. He *was* handling money on the Sabbath after all! It seemed so unthinkable, Rose dropped her melon and ran off. She felt confused by her father's behavior, which seemed to go against all that she had been taught.

Rose's father had changed more than his appearance. He had already begun to leave behind some of the religious and cultural customs of his homeland. Yet before long Rose would find herself becoming changed by America, too, in ways she could scarcely imagine.

✎ NEW CLOTHES ✐

After resting two days in the Segals' apartment, Marcus Ravage was no longer a guest. It was time for the greenhorn to get a job.

With the help of a cousin, Marcus began to look in the newspaper for jobs. He found ads from shops and factories and offices that seemed to

Jewish tailor shops

promise regular pay, and fine working conditions.

Then came the hard part. First, it often took him hours to even find the shops. Next he would stand in line with a hundred other applicants. But he was never chosen for the job. Marcus decided the only way to get a job was to have American clothes and look like an American, not a foreigner. Yet to buy American clothes he needed a job!

Many new immigrants, especially children and young people, were eager to change their heavy, foreign garb for American machine-made clothes as soon as they could. They didn't want to look like foreigners or to be teased for it.

One immigrant girl remembered, "I was such a greenhorn, you wouldn't believe. My first day in America I went with my aunt to buy some American clothes. She bought me a shirtwaist, you know, a blouse and a skirt, a blue print with red buttons and a hat, such a hat I had never seen. I took my old brown dress and shawl and threw them away. I know it sounds foolish, we being so poor, but I didn't care . . . When I looked in the mirror, I couldn't get over it . . . Just like an American."

Our initiation into American ways began with the first step on the new soil . . . [My father] told us not to lean out of the windows, not to point, and explained *the word "greenhorn." We did not want to be "greenhorns," and gave the strictest attention to my father's instructions.*

— MARY ANTIN

When Rose Cohen's eight-year-old brother arrived a year after she did, he was teased because of his heavy shoes, which had been made by the village shoemaker back home.

"Shoes more than any other article of clothing showed the 'green-horn'," Rose recalled, ". . . often he was so tormented by the children in the street that he would come into the house in tears."

Rose's family had no money for new, American-made shoes. But Rose's little brother had his own idea about how to get them. One day he came home after dark in his bare feet. He'd simply flung his shoes off a nearby tenement rooftop! He knew he'd be punished for throwing them away. But no matter what, he wanted to be sure his parents could never find those hated shoes again.

◇   ◇   ◇

ℬesides new clothing, many immigrants also adopted new names. Some friends helped Mary Antin's family exchange their traditional Jewish names for more American-sounding ones. Her mother's name wasn't easily translated, so she was given the name Annie. "Fetchke, Joseph, and Deborah became Frieda, Joseph, and Dora," Mary recalled.

Marcus Ravage was surprised at how easily people gave up their names. "It did not seem to matter at all what one had been called at home. The first step toward Americanization was to fall into one or the other of the two great tribes of Rosies and Annies."

Last names sometimes changed, too. Many people believe name changes took place when immigrants arrived at Ellis Island, by clerks who assigned new names. However, research by historians at the U.S. Immigration and Naturalization Service shows that name changes were more likely to take place over time, as last names were misspelled or simplified by teachers, employers, landlords, or immigrants themselves.

That's what happened to Leonard Covello. When Leonard brought home his first report card from school, his father noticed that the family's last name, Coviello, had been changed to Covello. He cried, "Leonard Covello! What happened to the 'i' in Coviello?"

Leonard explained that his teacher couldn't pronounce his name that way. Leonard didn't see what difference it made. "It's more American," he told his angry parents. "You just don't understand."

But to Leonard's parents, the family name represented honor and tradition. Although their new, Americanized name stuck, Leonard couldn't help complaining about his parents' attitude to his friend, Mary Accurso, another Italian immigrant.

Mary only smiled and said, "Maybe some day you will realize that *you* are the one who does not understand."

As Leonard would eventually realize, becoming an American did not mean he had to reject or belittle the traditions and customs of his homeland.

EVERYONE WORKED ON

Father, does everybody in America live like this? Go to work early, come home late, eat and go to sleep? And the next day again work, eat and sleep? Will I have to do that too? Always?

— ROSE COHEN

❧ MARCUS THE PEDDLER ❧

Sixteen-year-old Marcus Ravage was in trouble. No matter how he tried, he couldn't find a job. But Mrs. Segal, his relative (and now land-lady), didn't seem to think he was trying quite hard enough. It was time he began to earn his keep, she told him firmly. After all, he was sleeping in her apartment and eating her food.

Mrs. Segal gave Marcus a dollar and pushed him out onto the street to get started as a peddler. This was America, she reminded him, where "everybody hustled, and nearly everybody peddled."

Marcus was ashamed and nervous at the same time. A lowly peddler! This certainly wasn't the way he'd imagined his start in America. He'd been so sure he could get rich right away. But what other choice did he have?

So Marcus took Mrs. Segal's dollar and one of her nice brass trays to Orchard Street. There he bought two boxes of chocolates. Opening the boxes, he arranged the candy pieces on the tray. Now he was in business.

Marcus stood on a busy corner trying to catch the attention of the crowds rushing off to work. Marcus shivered. More than ever, he wished he'd brought his heavy winter coat.

A policeman chased him to another corner, where a boy ran by and tried to spill all his chocolates as a joke. And still, every person brushed by him without buying a thing. As the minutes went by, Marcus became even more cold and miserable. How could he face Mrs. Segal? Would she kick him out?

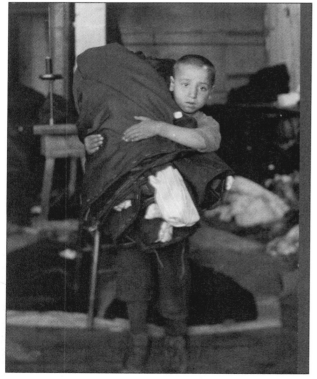

Boy with bundle of homework

After about two hours, Marcus noticed the streets beginning to fill with pushcarts and other peddlers. Marcus later remembered "peddlers with pushcarts and peddlers with boxes, peddlers with movable stands and peddlers with baskets, peddlers with bundles, with pails, with satchels and suitcases and trunks . . . They came pouring in from all directions — men with white beards, old women draped in fantastic shawls, boys with piping voices, young mothers with babes in their arms."

A man selling tablecloths nearby called out, "How is business?"

Marcus shook his head sadly. He hadn't

made a single sale. As it happened, the man was also from Romania, and he took Marcus under his wing. "Move along; elbow your way through the crowds in front of the stores, seek out the women with kids; shove your tray into their faces," the older man advised. "Don't be timid . . . And yell, never stop yelling: 'Candy, ladies! Finest in America. Only a nickel, a half-a-dime, five cents.'"

Then it was Marcus's turn to try. To his astonishment and delight, it began to work. His candy started to sell! By the end of the day, Marcus was glowing with pride.

That night Marcus went to a Romanian restaurant on Allen Street. For ten cents, he ordered the first meal he'd ever paid for in America: pot roast with mashed potatoes and gravy, and a dish of chopped eggplant with olive oil. While he ate, Marcus counted his earnings: seventy cents, not counting the chocolates he had eaten himself.

Marcus was on his way.

ROSE'S FIRST JOB

Soon after arriving in New York, twelve-year-old Rose Cohen had begun helping her father at his job at a garment shop, where he was paid by the piece. There had never been any question of Rose going to school. She had to help earn passage money to bring the rest of the family to America. And since every penny counted, sometimes that meant going without food.

Each morning when Rose went to help her father at the shop, a peddler came round with a basket. "Father used to buy me an apple and a sweetened roll," she remembered. "We ate while we worked . . . often I was almost sick with hunger."

As a growing girl, Rose needed extra food. But when she noticed her father scrimping to save money, Rose decided to sacrifice, too. She began to eat even less. "When as usual he gave me the apple and the roll, I took the roll but refused the apple."

By November, Rose had been in New York for several months and was still wearing a thin dress. One cold day her father took her to a second-hand clothing store on Division Street and bought "a fuzzy brown coat reaching a little below my waist, for fifty cents, and for himself a thin threadbare overcoat." They were ready for the winter.

They were ready for something else, too. Rose's father had found her a job of her own in a small sweatshop, sewing the linings of coat sleeves.

The night before her first day of work, Rose lay awake a long time, too nervous to sleep. What if the boss didn't like her? What if she couldn't do the work? Her father was counting on her. Rose couldn't bear to let him down.

In the morning Rose awoke before it was light. She wrapped her thimble and scissors and a piece of bread in a bit of newspaper. Carefully she stuck two needles into the lapel of her coat and set out through the dreary streets.

At the shop, Rose walked up a dark stairway. Suddenly the building's front door banged behind her, and she jumped. The hallway was so dark, she could barely see. Groping her way to the top, she felt for the door, pushed it open, and went into the sweatshop.

Everyone turned to stare at her. Some of the people sneered, and Rose heard a few low laughs. These grown-ups thought she was too young to do fine sewing. Rose squared her shoulders and went up to the boss. He handed her a coat to finish, and she slipped into a chair at the table.

"My hands trembled so that I could not hold the needle properly. It

Women in sweatshop

took me a long while to do the coat . . . I took it over [to] the boss and stood at the table waiting while he was examining it. He took long, trying every stitch with his needle. Finally he put it down and without looking at me gave me two other coats. I felt very happy!"

By evening, Rose's neck was stiff and her hands ached. "Seven o'clock came and everyone worked on. I wanted to rise as Father had told me to do and go home. But I had not the courage to stand up alone . . . I wished there were a back in my chair so that I could rest against it a little. When the people began to go home it seemed to me that it had been night a long time."

Messenger boy

The next morning Rose arrived promptly at seven o'clock only to find that everyone else was already there. The boss scolded her for being late, handed her two coats, and told her to hurry. From that day on, the boss always barked the same order: "Hurry!"

"I hurried but he was never satisfied," Rose said. ". . . Late at night when the people would stand up and begin to fold their work away, I too would rise feeling stiff in every limb and thinking with dread of our cold empty little room and the uncooked rice. He would come over with still another coat. 'I need it first thing in the morning,' he would give as an excuse.

"I understood that he was taking advantage of me because I was a child. . . . More tears fell on the sleeve lining as I bent over it than there were stitches in it."

✥ MAMMA, ARE YOU REALLY HERE? ✥

*B*esides working, Rose kept house for her father, washing, cleaning, and cooking. Many nights she put soup on to cook, only to fall asleep before it was ready, too tired to eat.

After months of work, the day came when her father counted out their savings and announced that at last they had earned enough to buy steamer tickets for the rest of the family. Rose was overcome.

"I could not realize that it was true, that we could send for them at once. I laid my arms on the table, buried my face in them and began to sob. Father laid his hand gently on my head. For once he did not scold me for my tears."

Rose and her father left their lodgings with the Felesbergs and rented a three-room apartment on Broome Street for seven dollars a month. One day Rose borrowed a pail and scrubbing brush and went to work, cleaning the floors of their new home. She scrubbed and rinsed for hours, changing the water often by carrying the pails of dirty water down the stairs to the yard and pumping fresh water. At last the grain of the wood

". . . the faster you work the more money you get. Sometimes in my haste I get my finger caught and the needle goes right through it. . . . I bind the finger up with a piece of cotton and go on working."
— SADIE FROWNE, garment worker

began to show. Feeling satisfied with her work, Rose sang a song made up on the spot: "Oh, how I'll scrub, how white our floors will be."

Later, when the men delivered their furniture, Rose tucked her dress up into her belt and ran around, showing them where to put each piece. In one room there was a big square table with six chairs, and two folding cots at the other end of the room. The big bed went into the bedroom. Rose longed for a third room, but this would have to do. When all was ready she and her father looked at one another and smiled happily.

At last the day came when the family was together again. Rose walked about in a happy dream. Often she leaned against her mother.

Shoeshine boy

Once, she asked, "Mamma, are you really here in America?"

Her mother hugged her gently and said, "Yes, all life is like a dream. Today we are here, tomorrow God knows...if only I had known I would be in America...I would have learned...how to write. Ah, if at least I could write to my mother!"

The family's problems weren't over. With seven mouths to feed, even the younger children had to help. "When the children came from school they would go out on the street and to the docks and pick up bits of coal, paper and wood and then we would make a fire," Rose recalled. "We used to put on water to boil and draw our chairs close to the stove, to draw all the warmth we could out of it."

Not long after, Rose's mother became ill. Rose and her father lost their jobs. Rose's eleven-year-old sister, Sarah, stepped in to help by baby-sitting.

Sometimes Rose would see her sister in the street, "wrapped in a woman's coat and carrying one little one on her back while two or three others were at her side. Her freckled small nose looked pinched, but she would look up so bravely with her soft gray eyes as she stood slightly bent under her burden. And in the evening she would bring home a few nickels."

Rose had to find another job quickly, too, until the busy season started once again in the garment shops. She left home to become a live-in maid for the Corloves, a family of six. Already weak and sickly from her time at the sweatshop, Rose was now expected to do all the daily household chores for a large family.

At dawn she carried coal from the cellar and made a fire in the stove for cooking and heating water. On wash days, Rose scrubbed clothes until her hands were chafed, rough, and red. Tuesdays and Wednesdays were ironing days. She also cleaned and washed floors on her hands and knees. Rose took care of the children and helped prepare meals, scaling fish, making barley noodles, or cleaning a chicken.

Mrs. Corlove was not very kind to the young girl. Rose was often sent to bed without supper while the rest of the family ate. If there were apples in a bowl on the table, Rose got the one with rotten spots on it.

At last Rose couldn't stand it anymore. She left to find work in a shop again. Anything, she decided, would be better than this job, where her every hour was marked night and day.

✌ CHILDREN AT WORK ✍

$\mathcal{R}$ose and her sister weren't alone. Many young immigrants had heavy work responsibilities because their parents couldn't find steady jobs that paid well enough to support their families. As one immigrant girl said, "In Italy girls don't work, but to eat here, everybody's got to work."

Children collecting wood scraps

A child's first job might be roaming the neighborhood streets

searching for pieces of wood for the stove, or following the coal cart to pick up any coal that dropped onto the street. Boys became shoe shiners, messengers, and newspaper boys. Young girls and women worked in factories that made everything from clothes and candy to caps and cigars, often getting paid no more than six or ten dollars a week. Most girls would bring their mothers their pay envelopes unopened, and receive a small allowance for spending money.

Child labor was a serious issue in New York. While exact figures are not known, experts believe that around 1880 there were probably 60,000 to 100,000 children between the ages of eight and sixteen working in New York City. Only about 35 percent of the state's children between five and twenty-one attended public schools.

Although several compulsory education and child labor laws were passed in New York State in the nineteenth century, the laws were difficult to enforce. The Compulsory Education Law of 1874 required children between the ages of eight and fourteen to attend school for fourteen weeks a year. School officials were supposed to visit the factories to check on children, but they had no time or budget to do so. In 1896, a new education law was passed that required children ages eight to twelve to go to school full time. Children between ages twelve and fourteen were required to go to school at least eighty days each year, and full time when not employed.

Many children who were not in school worked in factories, where they often inhaled harmful dust or fumes, had to stand or sit in uncomfortable positions for long hours, and risked injuries from accidents.

The Factory Act of 1886 prevented children under thirteen from working in factories (the age was raised to fourteen in 1889, where it stayed until 1935), but it didn't apply to stores or other types of businesses. There were only two inspectors hired to enforce the Factory Act of 1886, and by 1890, New York State had more than 65,000 factories.

In 1902, reformers such as Florence Kelley and Lillian Wald organized the Child Labor Committee to investigate the problem, expand awareness, and lobby for change. These efforts resulted in the Finch-Hill Act, which made employers responsible for illegally employed children for the first time, and also required that children under sixteen work less than nine hours a day. In an attempt to make the education and work laws coincide, in 1903 a bill was passed that required, among other things, that children stay in school up to the age of fourteen, when they could get working papers.

By 1900 the state of New York had nearly 80,000 factories employing over a million workers, with perhaps 50,000 to 75,000 of them under eighteen. It was impossible to inspect every factory, and the laws were only partially successful. It was not until the late 1930s that federal legislation established national standards for child labor.

Immigrant women often took in boarders to earn money. They also took jobs in many different kinds of factories and small shops. They worked long hours, making feathers and flowers, cigars, clothing, hats, paper boxes, and candy. Often the pay was extremely low. In one survey, an Italian girl who had left sixth grade earned $4.50 a week dressing dolls, an eighteen-year-old earned four dollars a week as a stock girl in a department store, while another young woman made four dollars a week packing nuts. Another woman, who had worked eighteen years hand-dipping chocolates, earned eight dollars a week, the same as a sixteen-year-old who had been doing the job for two years.

Immigrant men found work as laborers, carpenters, factory workers, cooks, barbers, watchmen, janitors, icemen, storekeepers, boatmen, stablemen, painters, bakers, butchers, printers, stonemasons, bootblacks, bartenders, street cleaners, bricklayers, and ragpickers. Others worked in the garment industry as cutters, cloak makers, tailors, pants makers, pressers, and cap makers.

Jewish immigrants from Russia and eastern Europe often had prior experience as tailors. Like Rose's father, they were able to find similar work in New York City in small sweatshops or larger factories.

Italian men most often had been laborers back home. In America they found work in construction jobs and as day laborers, with salaries of about six hundred to eight hundred dollars a year. The work was backbreaking and difficult. An Italian immigrant named Constantine Panunzio recalled that the first two words he learned when he arrived in America were "pick" and "shovel."

"I practiced for a day or two until I could say 'peek' and 'shuvle' to perfection," he later wrote. "Then I asked a fellow-boarder to take me to see what the work was like. . . . My heart sank within me, for I had thought it some form of office work. . . ."

> ⟩ ⟩ ⟩

Immigrants discovered that many jobs had a busy time and a slack time, when there was often no work at all. Since there was no unemployment system, people had no protection when they lost their jobs. If they didn't work, they had no money.

To help make ends meet, many families turned to "homework." This was not schoolwork, but work for pay done in the home. One of the most popular kinds of homework, especially in Italian immigrant families, was making artificial flowers for ladies' hats. Sometimes

A family making
artificial flowers

children only three or four years old helped make artificial flowers. In one survey of 371 home workers in 110 families, nearly half, or 181 workers, were children under sixteen. Children often helped their families make flowers after school, and sometimes stayed home to help finish orders.

In one family of seven, a three-year-old girl picked apart the violet petals, and her sister, age four, separated the stems, dipping an end of each into paste spread onto a piece of board on the kitchen table. The children's mother and grandmother then slipped the petals up the stems.

The pay for a gross (144) of flowers was ten cents. Working in a poorly lit kitchen from eight or nine in the morning until seven or eight at night, this family might finish twelve gross of flowers in a day, earning $1.20. In the busy season the family earned about $7.00 a week, but in the slack season, April to October, there was often no work.

WORKING IN THE GARMENT INDUSTRY

Fourteen hours a day you sit on a chair, often without a back . . . Fourteen hours with your back bent, your eyes close to your work you sit stitching in a dull room often by gas light. In the winter during all these hours as you sit stitching your body is numb with cold. In the summer, as far as you are concerned, there might be no sun, no green grass, no soft breezes. You with your eyes close to the coat on your lap are sitting and sweating the livelong day. The black cloth dust eats into your very pores. You are breathing the air that

all the other bent and sweating bodies in the shop are throwing off, and the air
that comes in from the yard heavy and disgusting with filth and the odor of
the open toilets.

— ROSE COHEN

Like Rose Cohen, Pauline Newman became a garment worker when she was a young girl. She began working at the Triangle Waist Company, a large shirtwaist factory in the Asch Building on Washington Place, when she was about thirteen. The Triangle Waist Company made shirtwaists, white blouses with full sleeves that were especially popular.

Pauline's workday began around seven-thirty in the morning and often didn't end until nine at night, especially in the busy season. The workers weren't paid for overtime. Most shirtwaist workers averaged fifty-six hours per week, working from eight until six during the week, and eight to five on Saturdays, with a half-hour lunch break at noon. Sometimes during the peak season the girls worked on Sundays, too.

Workers had few rights. They were fined for being five minutes late. They were charged for the use of lockers for their coats, for the needles they used, even for the power that made their sewing machines run.

Pauline recalled, "You were watched when you went to the lavatory and if in the opinion of the forelady you stayed a minute or two longer than she thought you should have you were threatened with being fired; there was the searching of your purse or any package you happened to have lest you may have taken a bit of lace or thread."

Pauline remembered a sign in the factory that read, IF YOU DON'T COME IN ON SUNDAY YOU NEED NOT COME IN ON MONDAY.

WILL IT EVER BE DIFFERENT?

One summer night as Pauline walked home from the factory, she felt overcome by despair. She saw little children playing in the gutter, men and women looking tired and drab, and the dark and filthy tenements.

Pauline went to her apartment and wrote about the drudgery of her work. "Every day the same foreman, the same forelady, the same shirt-waists, shirtwaists and more shirtwaists. The same machines, the same surroundings. The day is long and the task tiresome."

Pauline had one burning question: "In despair I ask, — dear God will it ever be different?"

Pauline sent her thoughts to the *Jewish Daily Forward,* a Yiddish newspaper read by many Jewish workers. She didn't think the words of an uneducated immigrant girl would be good enough to print. But a few days later Pauline's coworkers rushed up to congratulate her. The newspaper had published her piece.

Pauline felt a sense of excitement and accomplishment. This was the start of a lifelong journey for Pauline, who dedicated herself to helping others. ". . . In a small way I became the voice of the less articulate young men and women with whom I worked, and with whom later I was to join in the fight for improved working conditions and a better life for us all."

Of all the . . . underpaid workers in the city of New York, the worst paid are the unskilled workers in the tailor shops and among those the most mercilessly exploited are the women. Their work is tedious and exhausting, their hours are inhumanly long, their pay is ludicrously small, their shops are unattractive and filthy. As a rule these women are absolutely at the mercy of the employers, and the latter frequently treat them rudely, even cruelly.

— NEW YORK CALL, *January 3, 1910*

Garment workers on strike

$\mathscr{P}$auline wasn't the only young woman who yearned for change. In the fall of 1909, workers at several garment factories in New York turned to work stoppages, or strikes, to protest their working conditions. Many joined a union, Local 25 of the International Ladies' Garment Workers' Union. But the powerful factory owners hired thugs to harass the strikers and kept their factories open by bringing in workers willing to cross the picket lines.

On November 22, 1909, workers gathered at a huge meeting at the Cooper Union

Building to decide what to do. The union leaders didn't think a general strike of all working women had much chance of success. After all, most of the workers were Jewish and Italian immigrant girls, still in their teens.

Then came one of the most dramatic moments in American labor history. A young union organizer and worker named Clara Lemlich made her way through the crowd. Climbing up onto the platform, she looked out over the sea of faces.

Her black eyes flashing, Clara electrified the crowd with her simple plea: "I have listened to all the speakers. I would not have further patience for talk . . . I move that we go on a general strike!"

The next morning, 15,000 to 20,000 shirtwaist workers walked off their jobs in what was the largest strike by women up to that time. The strike became known as "The Uprising of the Twenty Thousand." The shirtwaist workers were fighting for raises, a shorter work week, better safety conditions, and no more than two hours of overtime each day.

Throughout that cold fall, the strikers were harassed and beaten as they stood shivering on the picket lines. Hundreds were arrested, and many families went hungry. But the factory owners were so powerful that when the strike ended on February 15, 1910, the results were mixed. Although not all of the workers' demands were met, the Uprising of the Twenty Thousand laid the groundwork for future successes in the garment industry. Through tremendous sacrifice and hard work, these young women were beginning to shape the future of work in America.

At about twenty minutes to five on the afternoon of Saturday, March 25, 1911, Rosey Safran, a worker at the Triangle Waist Company, was getting ready to leave the factory for the day. Suddenly, Rosey heard someone cry, "Fire!"

The Triangle Waist Company was located on the eighth, ninth, and tenth floors of the ten-story Asch Building, on the corner of Washington Place and Greene Street. The bell was just ringing to mark the close of the day.

In another few minutes, the workers would have been gone.

The fire probably began when someone on the eighth floor threw a cigarette into a rag bin. The flames spread rapidly to large cutting tables and the tissue paper patterns for the shirtwaist blouses that hung nearby.

Rosey Safran ran for the door on the Washington Place side of the building. She recalled, "The door was locked and immediately there was a great jam of girls before it. The fire was on the other side, driving us away from the only door that the bosses had left open for us to use in going in or out. They had the doors locked all the time for fear that some of the girls might steal something.

"... the flames were already blazing fiercely and spreading fast," said Rosey. "... Some girls were screaming, some were beating the door with their fists, some were trying to tear it open...."

The force of the heat and flames drove some of the girls to the windows. To the horror of the crowd below, they began to jump to their

"The whole door was a red curtain of fire . . . I ran out through the Greene Street side door, right through the flames."
— KATE ALTERMAN,
*Triangle Waist
Company worker*

deaths. The fire escape ladders reached only to the sixth floor. The firemen's nets were no help, either.

Although the Asch Building was supposedly "fireproof," it had no sprinklers. It had one inadequate fire escape, which collapsed, sending the people on it to their deaths. Although the fire was brought under control in about half an hour and the building itself didn't suffer much damage, the human toll was incredible. In less than thirty minutes, 146 workers died.

THE BEGINNING OF CHANGE

The Triangle factory fire tragedy shocked the people of New York. At a packed memorial on April 2, 1911, union organizer Rose Schneiderman insisted that giving money to the victims' families was not enough. She urged people to take action to improve conditions.

After the Triangle fire, the New York State Factory Investigating Commission was formed. It was headed by Robert Wagner and Al Smith, who later became

Victims of the Triangle fire

Thousands gather in the rain

governor of New York. As a result of the commission's investigation of working conditions in factories, the New York State Legislature eventually passed extensive reform laws.

On April 5, 1911, a dark, rainy day, more than 120,000 people marched through the streets of New York City in honor of seven unidentified victims of the Triangle factory fire.

Pauline Newman never forgot that day. Years later she said, "It seemed that the entire city was on the march. It was raining, but nobody cared, everybody went anyhow....I don't think we will ever forget it. Thousands of people stood in the rain, watching.... And it was pouring. Nature was weeping."

Garment workers at funeral march

On the Streets: Pushcarts, Pickles, and Play

I loved to wander the streets of the Lower East Side and get lost in the adventure.
The noisy bustling crowds fascinated me, everyone so feverishly busy.

— *Maurice Hindus*

SIGHTS, SOUNDS, AND SMELLS

Maurice Hindus was fourteen when he came to New York from a small village in Russia. He'd never lived in a big city before, and he looked around in wonder at everything he saw. So many men, women, and children, from so many different places!

As he walked through the teeming streets, Maurice was bursting with questions: Where did all these people come from? What did they talk about at home? What did they eat? Maurice was eager to talk to all these strangers, but he couldn't. He didn't speak any English.

"I contented myself with watching and wondering about them — the Chinese in the laundries, the Negroes as day laborers, the Irish as truck drivers, policemen and saloonkeepers, the Italians as shoe-shiners, ice and coal carriers, peanut vendors and organ-grinders," Maurice said.

Maurice was Jewish, but he loved to wander through the Italian neighborhoods. Often he caught sight of an Italian organ-grinder with a wizened-faced monkey strolling down Elizabeth Street or Mott Street, trailed by a group of dancing children. He liked to watch the children give pennies to the monkey, who took the coins with "a solemn doff of his tiny red cap."

Maurice couldn't help being tempted by the Italian stands and push-carts, spilling over with beautiful fruits and vegetables arranged not just as food for poor immigrants but as "works of art created to delight the passer-by."

Women selling vegetables

Closer to home was Hester Street, with its bustling Jewish market crowded with stalls and pushcarts. Here Maurice could find everything from food to household goods to books. Men stood on street corners or pushed through the crowds crying out their wares, "Needles! Thread! Shoelaces! Socks!"

Maurice watched customers and vendors squabble over prices while shopkeepers tried to cajole passers-by to come inside their stores. "All was bedlam, a cacophony of voices, the Yiddish dialects of Eastern Europe rising above all others."

✌ CHILDREN AND PLAY ☙

*I*n the midst of this noisy confusion, young children ran up and down, their mothers watching from tenement stairs and windows. Boys and girls followed the coal cart or roamed the alleys looking for scraps of wood for fuel.

"There were no parks at the time," remembered Dr. Robert Leslie, who was born in 1885 on the Lower East Side, the first of twelve children of a Russian Jewish immigrant who married a Scottish sailor. "Orchard and Ludlow were tenements one on top of the other with back houses . . . The only recreation was to go down to the East River where the barges were. The people would swim in it, but they also moved their bowels there."

When he was a boy on the Lower East Side, Russian immigrant Samuel Chotzinoff spent as much time as he could outside. "We would play in the sidewalks and in the gutter until the air grew dark and we could barely tell who was who. Sometimes we played hide-and-seek among the tenement houses. Then the lamplighter would emerge from

Playing leapfrog

the Bowery, carrying his lighted stick in one hand and a small ladder in the other. In the light of the gas lamps we played leapfrog over the empty milk cans in front of the grocery store." Some boys, Samuel remembered, could jump over seven cans at a time.

Children on the street jumped rope and played marbles and team games. Hopscotch and baseball were popular. But children for the most part had few toys and played with whatever was at hand. When Samuel and his family moved into their Stanton Street tenement apartment one hot August morning, he couldn't help staring at a large black horse lying dead in the gutter in front of their house. The stench was awful, and the horse was covered with a swarm of flies.

Later that day Samuel saw several boys sitting on top of the horse, trying to skin it with their pocketknives. They didn't realize it wasn't healthy for them to play with a decaying carcass. Luckily, a large van arrived before long and took the horse away.

When Samuel was about to enter third grade, his family moved to East Broadway, near Rutgers Square, which had a fountain. Even though it wasn't allowed, Samuel and his friends liked to take off their shirts and play in the water. One boy would stand guard, and when the lookout cried, "Cheese it! The cops!" everyone would scramble out of the fountain and scatter.

Samuel and his friends never ran out of things to do. They followed parades, organ-grinders, and horsecars. They chased after ambulances and fire trucks. "Fires broke out constantly in all seasons, and the air was seldom free from the clang of the fire engines, the shrieks of the siren and the clatter of the horses on the cobblestones. Following the fire engines could take up all your free time if you wanted it to."

Samuel and his friends also liked to play tag high up on tenement

Playing stickball

Playing London Bridge

roofs, hopping from one roof to another. Some buildings were taller than others, so often they had to jump down ten or twelve feet to the next roof. The danger, Samuel remembered, just added to the fun.

◅ CULTURE, POLITICS, AND YIDDISH THEATER ▻

The streets of the Lower East Side were more than a marketplace and a place for children to play. They were also the center of a community, where people gossiped, looked for work, and exchanged ideas about current events, politics, religion, and labor unions. In the Italian neighborhoods, men often gathered to socialize in the streets, as well as in cafés, candy shops, billiard halls, five-cent vaudevilles, puppet shows, and barbershops.

Italian women also led active social lives and formed close communities where families looked out for one another. Mothers often kept watch over children from their front stoops. Women met friends on the streets as they did daily errands or shopped for food in the markets. The streets were a place to exchange news and create a social network. As one writer has said, "The true heart of the Lower East Side beat in the streets. . . ."

Labor organizer Pauline Newman got her start as a public speaker on workers' rights by giving speeches on street corners. Without radios or television, she recalled, the only way to reach numbers of people was to get an American flag and a soapbox, and go from corner to corner.

"[The streets] . . . were my first American school."
— MAURICE HINDUS

A popular form of entertainment for eastern European immigrants was the Yiddish theater, which thrived on the Lower East Side. Beginning in the 1890s, the actor Jacob Adler became famous for his memorable roles in such plays as *The Jewish King Lear (Der Yiddisher Koenig Lear),* adapted by the playwright Jacob Gordin from Shakespeare's *King Lear.*

Samuel Chotzinoff never forgot the first time he went to a play, an adaptation of Shakespeare's *Hamlet* in Yiddish. Before the play began, Samuel looked around in wonder at the crowded theater, with candy and fruit and beer vendors threading through the aisles selling their wares. The orchestra played an overture, then the lights went out. As the curtain rose, a hush fell on the audience. Samuel held his breath.

"The play was about to begin, and I was overcome with emotion," Samuel remembered. Suddenly, "a faint, sickly yellow light pierced the surrounding gloom and disclosed an eerie figure . . . I knew only too well that I was looking at a ghost. . . .

"'Gamlet,' it said distinctly, in Yiddish, 'I am your father's ghost.' And with Hamlet I listened, with mounting horror."

⚜ PICKLES AND PRETZELS ⚜

Each street had its own favorite flavor. If the tang of herring was missing from Hester Street, the Hester Streeters thought they were walking in a vacuum . . . the Italian quarter had its air pockets filled with garlic. . . . If one walked down Orchard Street toward Rivington, one knew definitely that here air was literally cheese. . . .

— *EDDIE CANTOR, actor*

Immigrants encountered many new foods in New York. Soon after Maurice Hindus arrived, he had his first taste of the strange-looking

Pickles for sale

yellow fruit shaped like a long finger, the banana! He didn't especially like it.

But as a poor boy on the Lower East Side, Eddie Cantor often felt tempted to steal bananas when he was hungry. He learned to slip a banana up his sleeve while the peddler was busy filling some housewife's market bag.

"I got so that I could gulp a banana at one swallow and appear absolutely famished with a plum in each cheek," he said.

And, of course, there were pickles and pretzels. When Sophie Ruskay, whose parents owned a garment shop, went to the market with her mother, she had a hard time deciding what to choose. "At first I was tempted by the pungent-smelling pickles swimming in a barrel of brine, but instead I selected a huge pretzel, thickly sprinkled with coarse salt, which, with dozens more, hung at one end of the apple woman's cart."

People shopped frequently because they did not have refrigerators to store food. Some families did have iceboxes, though. One Lower East Side resident remembered delivering ice with his father. "My father would yell, 'Ice!' . . . People would come to the wagon and buy it. We would chop it in cakes, a piece for a cent, a bigger piece for two cents. In some cases we got an extra penny if we had to carry it up to the fourth floor or the fifth floor."

Immigrants were often astounded by what was available in the markets compared with their choices back home. When Maurice Hindus was a young boy in Russia, sugar had been a

Bread seller

luxury enjoyed by wealthy merchants or landlords. But in America, sugar was so cheap, Maurice could sweeten his tea with as much as he liked and his mother wouldn't scold him.

And then there was white bread. At first Maurice couldn't get enough of it: "...sweet rolls, plain rolls, with cinnamon and poppy seeds, without cinnamon and poppy seeds. I ate them during meals and between meals," he recalled. Eventually, though, he found himself missing the thick, black bread he had loved back home.

Like sugar and white bread, meat was more readily available in America. Samuel Chotzinoff loved his mother's Friday

Pushcart on Mulberry Street

evening Sabbath dinners, complete with soup, a stuffed fish, roasted meat, potatoes, gravy, and carrots. Samuel's father was fond of calf's foot jelly, which his mother would cool on the fire escape of their tenement apartment. But the family's Friday night feasts, Samuel remembered, were only possible by saving up during the rest of the week, when he often went hungry.

Samuel's parents ran a delicatessen for a short time, and his mother cooked the meat for the store. Samuel would stand beside her in a large, sunless room as she cooked "corned beefs, tongues, and pastramis in a tin clothes-boiler over a three-burner gas stove. When she lifted the lid of the boiler, the fatty, bubbling water spilled over on the floor. . . ."

Even if Samuel had just finished lunch or dinner, he always begged for a slice of meat. He liked to eat it plain, without even a slice of bread.

Boy selling bread

In Avigliano there were times when there was no food in the house. Then we bolted the door and rattled kitchen utensils and dishes to give the impression to our close neighbors that the noonday meal was going on as usual. . . . In America it was not much different. Our people had the worst jobs — jobs that paid little and were very uncertain. . . . My mother lived in constant fear from the uncertainty of life.

— LEONARD COVELLO

Immigrants brought with them not only language and culture, but food traditions, too. In general, Italians preferred a diet of macaroni and dried beans, as well as cheese, bread, and fresh vegetables such as onions, cabbage, and greens. Jewish families ate herring, fresh fish, meats, potatoes, carrots, cabbage, and beets.

No matter what their nationality, families often struggled to get enough to eat during hard times. Sammy Aaronson, who grew up on the Lower East Side, recalled that "meat soup was a big thing and we sometimes could have it once a week. Outside of that, the only hot food we ever had was potatoes. I never tasted anything like steak or roast beef or lamb chops until I was sixteen years old. We lived on pumpernickel, herring, bologna ends and potatoes. The whole family could eat for fifteen or sixteen cents a day, sometimes less. . . .

"We paid a penny a herring and two took care of the whole family. Another penny bought three pounds of potatoes. We always had the meat soup on Friday nights. It was made up of leftovers and ends and bones which the butcher sold for six cents a pound instead of throwing away. Three pounds was plenty for a meal for us."

In a study published in 1907, immigrant families from Ireland, eastern Europe, Italy, and other places were asked to keep track of their monthly living expenses. This study helps us understand how families lived and what they spent on rent, food, clothes, and medicine.

One family in the study consisted of an Italian stonecutter, his wife, and four children. The family usually did better in the summer months. Then the father might earn four or five dollars a day. But because the work was not steady, during the winter the father worked in an artificial flower factory, earning only nine or ten dollars a week.

Here are the food costs for this Italian family of six in February 1904:

MONTHLY EXPENSES

FOOD	COST
Soup meat, veal, ham	$7.13
Chicken and fish	$3.25
Butter and cheese	$2.21
Eggs and milk	$2.43
Vegetables and salad greens	$2.21
Dried beans and chestnuts	$1.23
Potatoes	$0.90
Bread	$2.81
Sugar	$0.67
Coffee	$0.35
Macaroni	$2.07
Cereal (rice, barley)	$0.69
Fruit	$0.10
Olive oil	$0.70
Other	$0.65
Total	$27.40

Food prices might seem low compared with today's, but the total yearly income for this family of six was about $690. After paying for food, heat, and rent, immigrant families like this one had little money left over for clothes, furniture, magazines and books, entertainment, insurance, or medical bills. Usually the mother of the family handled the budget.

Families did their best to create a comfortable home. More expensive items, like furniture, were often purchased "on time." They were paid for little by little, on an installment plan. Sewing machines, which cost from twenty-five to sixty dollars, were usually paid for at the rate of one dollar a week. Some families even scrimped and saved to buy pianos for their children, which cost about three hundred dollars. At ten dollars a month, it would take more than two and a half years to pay for them.

Samuel Chotzinoff recalled that his mother once bought a flowered

Marketplace on Hester Street

silk tablecloth for ten weekly payments of twenty-five cents each, even though the family was already struggling to pay for food, rent, and to put quarters in the gas meter. And when ten-year-old Samuel came home one day and told his mother he longed to take piano lessons for ten cents a lesson, she agreed to help him. Samuel grew up to become a musician.

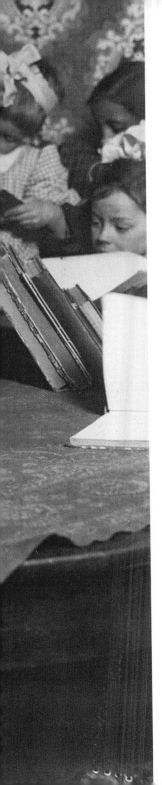

A New Language, A New Life

We had to visit the stores and be dressed from head to foot in American clothing; we had to learn the mysteries of the iron stove, the washboard, and the speaking-tube; we had to learn to trade with the fruit peddler through the window, and not to be afraid of the policeman; and above all, we had to learn English.

— MARY ANTIN

ABOVE ALL, WE HAD TO LEARN ENGLISH

After two weeks of peddling, Marcus Ravage traded in his chocolates for toys. Toys, at least, wouldn't spoil if he couldn't sell them right away. Soon Marcus was earning enough to pay his landlady, Mrs. Segal, fifty cents a week for his bed. Not only that, he was usually able to treat himself to a hot evening meal at his favorite Romanian restaurant on Allen Street. The bustling restaurant felt warm and cozy after a day spent outside on the cold streets.

Here, Marcus made friends with other Romanian immigrants. They shared news from back home, and tried to make sense of this strange new place and language. Sometimes a musician would play and sing an old, familiar song, and Marcus would join in. More than once he had to wipe away a tear, thinking of his parents back home.

For a while, Marcus was satisfied with his life. Then he began to notice boys his own age speaking English and carrying heavy stacks of books. These boys, Marcus realized, were going to school.

Marcus decided he didn't want to be a peddler all his life. He found a regular job in a tailor shop. There he was surprised to find that his coworkers brought books to read on their short lunch breaks. In the evenings they attended night school, or lectures at the Educational Alliance.

An important part of the Lower East Side, the Educational Alliance was a center for culture and education, offering concerts, art exhibits, lectures, and a wide variety of classes in everything from English and Yiddish to music and sewing. Russian immigrant Abraham Hyman recalled the vibrant atmosphere in the Jewish community: "You have to consider the spirit of the East Side. . . . There were educational clubs. Everyone was reading newspapers and reading books. The spirit itself was electric — ambition to get out of this poverty."

Encouraged by his new friends, Marcus began to venture out to lectures, too. Then he enrolled in night school, studying English, German, and algebra.

It wasn't easy to go to night school after working long hours in the shop. "I cannot tell you how we did it," Marcus later wrote. "I only remember that I would sit and puzzle over x's and y's from the time I got home at eleven o'clock until my eyes would give out; and at seven in the morning I would be back at the machine sewing shirts. . . ."

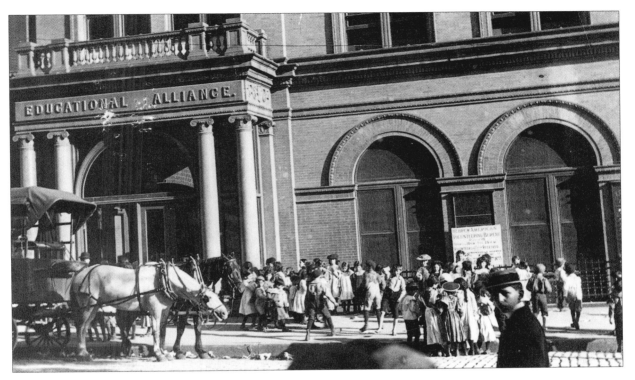

The Educational Alliance

⤷ PAGE BY PAGE ↝

ℛussian immigrant Maurice Hindus had to learn English more quickly than most. Soon after he arrived in New York, he found a job as an errand boy in a shop. One of his duties was to order lunches for the girls who worked there. And the girls gave their orders in English.

On his first day, an Italian girl named Lina showed him how to write down the orders and go to a nearby lunch counter to buy the food. Maurice followed along in a daze. How was he ever going to get it right? He could barely speak a word of English, let alone write it.

The next day, Maurice took the lunch orders alone. He tried to write them down as best he could, some words in Russian and some phonetically. But when he read off the lunch order, the large, stern man behind the counter began to shoot questions at him so fast, Maurice could only shrug. The man snatched the paper from Maurice's hand, stared at it in confusion, scowled, and began to fill the orders.

Children's Aid Society

Maurice brought the lunches back and handed them out. When the girls opened their packages, they began to laugh and yell and complain, exchanging sandwiches, cakes, and pies and wanting to know where their missing items were.

Maurice felt like giving up. But Lina's mother called him to her worktable, gave him a piece of cake, and mumbled in sympathy, "Goota boy, goota boy."

At last, giggling and teasing, Lina taught him some basic words so he could do the job. Maurice learned quickly. "In less than a week I could go about and take orders by myself and write them down in English and only rarely get them so badly mixed that the girl who ordered a frankfurter without mustard received a corned-beef sandwich with mustard."

And what did Maurice buy when he first got paid? A Russian-English dictionary! Maurice bought a novel and began to try to read it. Each time he saw a word he didn't know, he copied it on a piece of paper. After he finished each page, he looked up the words he didn't know in his new dictionary, then read the page again until he could understand it.

Maurice did this, page by page, until he finished the book. It was slow going, but he didn't give up. "Every day more of the strange sounds took on meaning as words arranged themselves into sentences."

✆ A NEW ADVENTURE ✆

By the time Maurice Hindus had been in New York a year he had taught himself English, spending countless hours at the library and attending many lectures. More than anything, he wanted to go to high school. But would an American high school let him in?

Maurice went to see Dr. Frank Rollins, principal of Stuyvesant High School. Maurice waited anxiously in the waiting room. His heart was pounding so hard, he felt sure Dr. Rollins would be able to hear it.

Maurice didn't think he had much of a chance of getting into school. Although he'd completed elementary school in Russia, he'd never attended school in America. He would probably be asked to take an entrance exam in English. Could he pass it?

"I trembled all over as I went into Dr. Rollins' private office," Maurice remembered. Dr. Rollins greeted him with a broad smile. He talked to Maurice about his studies, then asked him to write out some answers to questions in English.

When Maurice finished, he passed the paper to Dr. Rollins and watched anxiously as the principal read it. After a few long minutes, Dr. Rollins looked up and smiled. Maurice, he said, was welcome to start school on Monday.

"My head swam with triumph," said Maurice. He could attend high school in America! "Nobody had asked a single question about my family's social standing, economic condition, or religion; tuition would be free, books, too, would be supplied. I strode down the street feeling as though I had suddenly entered into a new life and a new adventure."

Jewish school in Hester Street tenement

✃ RUSH, RUSH, RUSH ✄

Although a free public education was one of the benefits of living in America, many immigrant families couldn't make ends meet without at least some of their children working either full or part time. Instead of playing sports in his new high school, Maurice Hindus took a job as an errand boy in the afternoons. Leonard Covello had begun working when he was only twelve, delivering bread for a bakery before school.

Leonard's job started at four-thirty each morning. After gulping down a roll and some coffee mixed with milk, he made his way through the empty streets, pulling a wagon made from an old packing crate and baby carriage wheels.

Leonard wanted to carry a lantern, but it was too hard to manage along with the bags of bread. So often he would find himself in dingy, dim apartment buildings where he had to grope along, banging into walls, stepping on cats, and hearing rats scurry out of the way. And he always kept a wary eye out for janitors' dogs.

"It was rush, rush, back and forth from the bakery until all the orders were delivered," Leonard remembered. "Then I had to run home and get ready for school. For this work I received one dollar and seventy-five cents a week. It was not very much but it helped a great deal when meat was twelve cents a pound and milk six cents a quart."

Sometimes Leonard felt like giving up. But then he would see his father come home exhausted from work, night after night. "In me you see a dog's life," Leonard's father said. "Go to school. Even if it kills you."

❧ NIGHT SCHOOLS ☙

I don't like the work I'm doing now. . . . holding the scissors all day; the scissors hurt my hand so, and it's so tiresome cutting all the time. But it was worse when I was at children's caps, on my feet all day. . . . But I can't stop night school because I'm tired, if I want to get my education. I want to go to evening high [school] and be a stenographer.

— FOURTEEN-YEAR-OLD GIRL, 1914

In some immigrant families, the older children worked so younger brothers or sisters could attend school. Most children left school at fourteen to get working papers. Since most girls at this time were expected to marry rather than pursue careers or go to college, they often had to leave school early to work and help support the family.

Working girls sometimes enrolled in night classes. In addition to English, night schools offered classes in cooking, dressmaking, millinery (making hats), typewriting, stenography, and bookkeeping. Classes for boys and men included such trades as blacksmithing, cabinet making, carpentry, plumbing, printing, and engineering.

But even night school wasn't always possible. ". . . Going to night school was a question of working overtime or going to school," Pauline Newman recalled. "And the overtime won out."

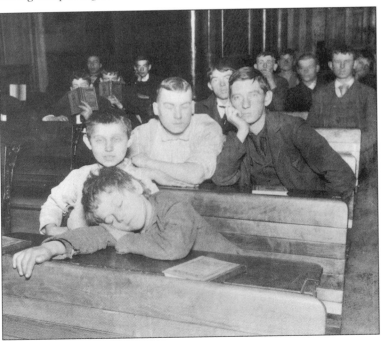

Falling asleep in night school

Still, Pauline wanted to learn English. She had managed to learn the alphabet, but couldn't read very well. She made up her mind to teach herself, so from one of the pushcarts she bought Charles Dickens's novel *Great Expectations* for a nickel.

"And every night I read a page," Pauline said. "By reading, that's how you learn English. . . . It's a slow process, but you learn. I happened to want this thing enough to stick with it."

Although Pauline couldn't pursue a formal education, living on the Lower East Side meant she had opportunities to attend lectures on art, literature, and politics. As Pauline became involved in labor unions and in Socialist politics, her circle expanded. She began to make friends who spoke English instead of Yiddish.

Pauline Newman didn't give up because she had a goal. She wanted to learn to speak and read English not just for her own benefit, but to help thousands of her fellow workers in the fight for better conditions.

"After working all day . . . I sat down in the classroom. It was so nice and warm . . . I just fell asleep. I started to snore something terrific . . . the teacher came over and shook me. . . . And that was the beginning, or the end, of my formal education in this country."
—ABRAHAM GAMBERG

❧ CHILDREN, SCHOOLS, AND PARENTS ❧

A child that came to this country and began to go to school had taken the first step into the New World. But the child that was put into the shop remained in the old environment with the old people, held back by the old traditions, held back by illiteracy.

— ROSE COHEN

› › ›

As young immigrants learned English, met new people, and adopted American customs, they sometimes felt caught between the world of their parents and their new world. At school, American teachers didn't always understand the backgrounds and cultures of immigrant children. Often the child's first language and culture were viewed as inferior.

Leonard Covello recalled that none of his elementary school teachers talked about Italy, the Italian language, or famous Italians except for Columbus. "We soon got the idea that Italian meant something inferior, and a barrier was erected between children of Italian origin and their parents."

Leonard was careful to keep his school life separate from his home. When he met new American friends, he didn't invite them home because he didn't want them to see his parents or how they lived. And he never wanted his mother to meet his teachers. He felt embarrassed that she didn't speak English and still dressed like a foreigner.

"If I could read the whole world of knowledge was open to me."
—Rose Cohen

Leonard and his friends didn't share problems at school or in the streets with their parents, either. "How could parents understand?" he later wrote. "Parents belonged in one of the many separate watertight compartments of the many lives we lived in those days."

Once, in high school, Leonard took second prize in a physical education chinning contest. Although he was small, his arms were strong from hard work. Leonard was so proud of his achievement, he couldn't resist sharing the news at dinner. But he didn't get the reaction he expected.

Leonard's father threw down his napkin and, in a burst of anger, cried, "There is hardly enough to eat in the house. We kill ourselves. . . .

We work so that he can have some future — and he spends his time at school playing!"

Leonard tried to explain that physical education was part of school. His father only became angrier, saying that if all Leonard cared about was playing, or being a strong man, he should stop school and go to work. His father was sacrificing so Leonard could learn and get a good job someday, not so Leonard could spend his time playing in school.

Physical education

Usually Leonard just shouted, "You don't understand!" But this time he was so upset, he ran to his friend Mary's house without a word.

It was not important how strong he was, Mary reminded Leonard. The important thing was that the contest had made him feel better. "You're just as good as the next fellow. That's what you should have explained to your mother and father."

But his father's words had thrown Leonard into despair. Maybe his

Girls' physical education

father *was* right. Leonard loved learning, but what was the use of going to school when his family needed money so badly? Where would school get him, anyway? A poor Italian boy like him would never have enough money to go to college.

And so, at the end of his third year of high school, Leonard Covello quit school.

Looking to the Future: Will It Ever Be Different?

I knew it existed, a vast shimmering, mysterious world . . . stretching beyond New York to the Pacific Ocean, and here was I cooped up in the tenement section of the Lower East Side, with not a glimmer of a chance to make its acquaintance.

— Maurice Hindus

⚚ TAKING A CHANCE ⚚

Leonard Covello walked into the school office and turned in his books. No one asked why he was quitting. No one seemed to care.

Outside, some of his friends patted him on the back as if he'd just been released from prison. They couldn't understand why he had tears in his eyes.

Leonard took a job loading and unloading crates from horse-drawn wagons. At first his hands got so sore and blistered, he had to soak them each night in warm water. Before long, though, they became callused and rough from the hard work.

Although Leonard was helping his family, in his heart he felt restless. He borrowed books from the library to read at night. He slept near the window so he could catch the first morning light and read without disturbing his two brothers, who slept in the same bed. Leonard seemed so unhappy that his friend Mary Accurso kept trying to persuade him to go back to school. Mary was the first girl Leonard knew from his part of Italy who had gone to college and become a teacher.

After working for a year, Leonard decided to return to school. He joined the debate society and wrote for the school paper. Yet as high school graduation approached, Leonard's doubts returned. What next? One of his best friends was going to Columbia University and he urged Leonard to try for college.

"College costs money. Money I haven't got," Leonard told Mary. "Money I will never have. Money. Money. Money. I'm so sick of the sound of that word."

Mary reminded him that people with less money had gone to college. "It's all in how much you want to go. . . ."

Leonard just didn't see how it would be possible.

WHAT ABOUT LOVE?

Rose Cohen was looking to the future, too. When she was sixteen, a matchmaker arranged for her to meet a young grocer in the neighborhood. Her parents and the young man urged Rose to marry. The young man had his own successful grocery store. He would be able to take care of Rose.

Rose knew that if she refused, her father would blame her for missing a chance to better things for all of them. After all, if Rose married a grocer, her family would be able to buy potatoes, sugar, and bread at a discount.

Rose had met the young man just once. Now she was being asked to decide her future. Rose couldn't help wonder: *But what about love?*

✤ THE PROMISE OF GOLDEN DREAMS ✤

As young immigrants like Leonard and Rose grew up, they often found themselves asking the same question Pauline Newman had wondered: "Will it ever be different?"

What would their futures bring? Leonard Covello dreamed of going to college. Marcus Ravage did, too. Rose Cohen, who had never attended school in America, simply wished to learn English well enough to read literature. Maurice Hindus longed to leave New York and experience the American countryside. Pauline Newman was committed to working for the rights of workers.

More than anything, though, these immigrants and thousands more like them wanted to escape the poverty and endless toil they and their parents had known. They wanted to be free from, as Leonard Covello put it, "the monotonous day-in-day-out routine without any hope of change or hope for the future, without any sense of accomplishment." They wanted to find out what being an American could mean, and to discover, as Leonard's grandmother had once whispered, their own "golden dreams of the future."

But were those dreams within their reach?

✍ LEONARD ✍

One afternoon in 1907, Leonard Covello stood uncertainly by his English teacher's desk. Miss Harding had encouraged Leonard to try for a Pulitzer scholarship. The competition would be fierce, with hundreds of students across the city applying. The winning student would receive twenty-five dollars a month and free tuition at Columbia University.

As Leonard thought of the long months and years of backbreaking work stretched before him, he gathered his courage. "Is it too late — too late for the scholarship?" he asked.

Miss Harding smiled and assured him there was still time. "I'm glad. I'm glad that you decided to take a chance."

Leonard took his examinations for the Pulitzer scholarship. All summer, he waited for news.

Leonard's family was hoping for other good news that summer, too. Leonard's mother had fallen ill. But when at last the doctor came, he shook his head. There was nothing he could do.

One day when Leonard came home from work, his brother rushed to meet him at the door. Leonard's heart began to pound with fear. Was his mother worse?

Leonard rushed to the bedroom. His mother reached out her hands to him. Someone from the scholarship committee had come to visit, she told him with an excited smile. "Narduccio, my son. It has happened. You will go to college. You will!"

Leonard Covello's mother died before she was able to see her son enter Columbia University in the fall of 1907.

After his graduation from Columbia, Leonard began teaching Spanish, French, and Italian to high school students. He went on to complete his doctorate in education, focusing on Italian American children. In the early 1930s, there was a movement to build a trade school in his neighborhood of East Harlem. Leonard Covello was among those who argued that the new school, Benjamin Franklin High School, should be a regular, academic high school, offering the young people of East Harlem the same opportunities as other children.

Leonard Covello served as principal of Benjamin Franklin High School for twenty-two years, working tirelessly to instill in his students a love of learning and a belief in themselves. In his autobiography, *The Heart Is the Teacher,* Leonard said, "My pupils have always been a source of wonder and delight to me . . . I have loved and sought to understand them, finding in each face the suggestion and spark of something different and new."

Leonard Covello died in 1982 at the age of ninety-four.

> > >

$\mathcal{D}$espite pressure from her parents, Rose Cohen did not marry the grocer.

Instead, her health failed. Luckily for Rose, dedicated nurses like Lillian Wald at the Nurses' Settlement on Henry Street helped her get the hospital treatment she needed. They also arranged for her go to the countryside to rest.

Through Rose's experiences in the hospital, she began to hear English spoken by Americans. Eventually, she began to learn to read and take classes. She later married a tailor named Joseph Cohen and had one daughter.

Through the encouragement of her new friends, Rose began to write. Her autobiography, *Out of the Shadow: A Russian Jewish Girlhood on the Lower East Side,* was first published in 1918. Her book received positive reviews, and Rose began to meet other writers and artists. Unfortunately, little is known of Rose Cohen's later years. It appears that she died in her forties around 1925.

$\mathcal{M}$aurice Hindus had come to America from the Belorussian village of Bolshoye Bykovo in 1905, when he was about thirteen. The Jews in his town had been spared many of the atrocities that happened else-where in Russia, and Maurice always looked back on his childhood home with fondness. After three years in New York City he grew ill and tired of city life. He went to North Brookfield, a rural town in upstate New York, where he worked on a farm. Maurice attended Colgate University and went to graduate school at Harvard University. He later became a lecturer and journalist specializing in Russia, and was a sympathizer of the Socialist revolution there. He authored several books, including an autobiography, *Green Worlds*, published in 1938. He died in 1969.

✍ PAULINE ✍

Pauline Newman, a Lithuanian immigrant who first worked in the Triangle Waist Company at the age of thirteen in 1901, became one of the first women organizers for the International Ladies' Garment Workers' Union. During the shirtwaist strike in 1909, Pauline worked for the International Ladies' Garment Workers' Union raising money to help the strikers.

In the following years, Pauline traveled extensively for the cause of labor unions. She gave speeches, raised funds, and organized workers across the country. She also served on many federal Labor Department advisory committees during the 1930s and 1940s. The girl who had once been afraid her words were not good enough to publish went on to write many articles on issues important to working women.

Pauline Newman was deeply moved by the tragedy at the Triangle factory. She spoke at every annual memorial observance of the Triangle factory fire except for the seventy-fifth anniversary in 1986. She died in New York City two weeks following that anniversary, at around the age of ninety-eight.

✌◯ MARCUS ◯✍

Marcus Eli Ravage had come to America from Romania in 1900 at the age of sixteen. While working in a garment shop, he continued his education in night school, even though it meant his pay was reduced when he couldn't work overtime. He even had to pay fifty cents more a month for his room because he was burning more gas to study at midnight.

Nevertheless, Marcus persisted, eventually enrolling in high school and graduating. To his disappointment, he didn't win the scholarship he wanted. But that didn't stop him. He researched colleges around the country to find one he could afford. In the fall of 1906 he took a train to Columbia, Missouri, and enrolled at the University of Missouri, arriving with only seventeen dollars. He graduated in 1909 and went on to study at the University of Illinois and Columbia University, becoming a journalist and freelance writer. Marcus Eli Ravage was the author of several books, including his 1917 autobiography, *An American in the Making*. He died in 1965.

> > >

The immigrants who flooded New York in the late nineteenth and early twentieth centuries faced extreme poverty, prejudice, and difficult living conditions. Yet through determination, hard work, and sacrifice, many improved their economic situation within one or two generations. Some were able to move from unskilled manual labor to more skilled jobs. Many immigrants who started out at the bottom working at unskilled manual jobs began to move into better paying blue-collar jobs on the docks and in factories. Others moved into white-collar jobs in offices, retail stores, manufacturing, and professional positions.

In general, boys had more opportunities for higher education and for better paying jobs. Although more girls finished high school and obtained clerical positions, many women at this time were expected to stay home and raise children after marriage.

Throughout the early twentieth century, reformers worked to try to prohibit child labor and raise the age at which children left school to work. As families' incomes rose, children could stay in school longer, so that more could finish high school or even attend college. But that did not mean that "homework" such as artificial flower-making, which often involved young children, was eliminated. In fact, it was not until the 1930s, when laws were passed at the federal and state level, that home-work was prohibited. By September 1936, New York children were required to stay in school until they were sixteen years old. With some exceptions, sixteen has remained the legal working age through today.

Just as they took their first steps as "greenhorns" into the bustling marketplaces of the Lower East Side, the young people whose voices we hear in this book took their first steps as adults. Some remained in the neighborhoods of the Lower East Side, living and working and raising children of their own. Others took paths that led them outside the Lower East Side, away from their homes, parents, and community. Some found success beyond anything their parents could have imagined.

And while the young people whose stories we follow did change their social and family behaviors in America, they often were guided by, and kept hold of, their own ideals and values. In turn, our society has been imbued with the rich diversity of cultures, languages, and traditions immigrants have brought — and continue to bring.

ECHOES OF THE PAST

In the foreword to his 1949 autobiography, *A Dreamer's Journey,* Jewish immigrant Morris Raphael Cohen, a distinguished philosopher and professor at the City College of New York, gave some advice to his granddaughter. He asked her to try to understand what it was like for her great-grandparents (his parents), who had torn up their roots and come to America to make a better life for their children. By reading about their struggles as immigrants, Morris hoped his granddaughter would better understand their courage, hopes, and dreams.

Understanding is important, Morris Raphael Cohen said. For, he reminded his granddaughter, our lives are brief, and the things we make, whether ships or houses or governments, don't always last. But, wrote Cohen, "the echoes from soul to soul will go on so long as human life lasts."

Over the last several decades new immigrants have arrived on the Lower East Side from China, Hong Kong, Taiwan, Southeast Asia, Cuba, Puerto Rico, Mexico, the Dominican Republic, Nicaragua, El Salvador, and many other countries. Today's immigrants have many of the same needs and challenges as those of the previous centuries. They also cherish the same dreams of an education and better future for their children.

The Lower East Side is continually in flux. Walking through its streets today, you hear many languages and see men, women, and children from many different places. People from all over the world visit the Lower East Side Tenement Museum on Orchard Street to learn more about the lives of those who came here in the past. Chinatown and Little Italy bustle with tourists, shoppers, and restaurant-goers.

Yet if you stop on Hester or Mulberry or Orchard Street and listen closely, you can almost still hear the shouts of children playing tag on the tenement roofs, and the echoes of peddlers crying, "Candy! Finest in America!" Or even the soft footsteps of girls like Rose Cohen, rushing to work on a cold, dark morning.

AFTERWORD

IN A PHOTOGRAPH BY LEWIS HINE, AN IMMIGRANT MOTHER AND FOUR CHILDREN ARE SEATED AT A KITCHEN TABLE. THE ROOM IS DARK, AND though one window is visible, it's hard to tell whether it is day or night. An oil lamp flickers on the table, which is piled high with artificial petals to be strung into flowers for hats. The children are serious and silent at their work. The littlest one has tiny hands and full cheeks. She cannot be much more than five.

When I first saw this photograph, I was filled with curiosity to know more about what life was like for immigrant children and families like these. To learn more, I read many books and scholarly articles, visited the Lower East Side Tenement Museum and walked through the neighborhood streets, listened to oral history tapes, and pored over photograph collections in libraries, museums, and on the Internet.

In the end, what impressed me most was the diversity and richness of the immigrants' experiences. Listening to the voices and accounts of the

Lewis Hine
(George Eastman House / photograph
by Barbara Puorro Galasso)

people I have included in *Shutting Out the Sky* helps me appreciate once again the uniqueness of each human being.

The people in the old photographs in this book may seem nameless, part of a large wave of immigrants swept by historical circumstances from Russia, eastern Europe, or Italy, and brought together in New York City. Yet, as I hope some of the voices in this book reveal, each child's experience of family, culture, work, and the world was unique.

In our family, we always heard stories of our grandmother, who had immigrated alone from Ireland as a teenager. She was an invalid when I knew her, and died when I was young, without ever telling me her story. I hope this book will encourage you to find the stories in your own family.

TIMELINE

1860

Italian population in New York City
numbers approximately 1,500.

1880

United States population numbers
approximately 50 million.

Jewish population in New York City
numbers approximately 80,000.

1882

May Laws of 1882 place further
restrictions on Jews in Russia.

Chinese Exclusion Act prohibits
immigration of Chinese to the
United States.

1886

Factory Act of 1886 prohibits children
under thirteen from working in
U.S. factories. The age is raised to
fourteen in 1889.

1890

Jacob Riis publishes *How the Other
Half Lives*.

1892

Ellis Island immigration station
opens.

1897

Wooden buildings on Ellis Island
burn to the ground. The center
reopens in 1900.

1901

Tenement House Law of 1901 sets

better lighting, sanitation, fire, and
safety standards in tenement
buildings.

⇥ 1902 ⇤
Child Labor Committee is
organized.

⇥ 1907 ⇤
In a single day, more than 11,000
immigrants pass through Ellis
Island.

⇥ 1909 ⇤
Shirtwaist workers strike in the
"Uprising of the Twenty Thousand."

⇥ 1910 ⇤
Jewish population in New York City
numbers more than one million.
The Jewish population on the Lower
East Side peaks at close to 550,000
people.

⇥ 1911 ⇤
Fire at the Triangle Waist Company
on March 25 kills 146 workers.
In April, thousands participate in a
memorial march. Factory owners
Isaac Harris and Max Blanck are
acquitted of manslaughter in
December.

⇥ 1920 ⇤
Italian population in New York City
numbers approximately 400,000.
The Yiddish newspaper, the *Jewish
Daily Forward*, has a circulation
of nearly 250,000.

⇥ 1924 ⇤
Johnson-Reed Act, also called the
Immigration Act of 1924, sets
limits on immigration.

⇥ 1925 ⇤
Ellis Island closes.

FURTHER READING

$\mathcal{R}$eaders interested in learning more about the shirtwaist strike and the Triangle Waist Company fire will find Joan Dash's book, *We Shall Not Be Moved: The Women's Factory Strike of 1909* (New York: Scholastic Inc., 1996), and Mary Jane Auch's novel, *Ashes of Roses* (New York: Henry Holt and Company, 2002), of interest. Russell Freedman's *Kids at Work: Lewis Hine and the Crusade against Child Labor* (New York: Clarion Books, 1994) provides information about child labor. Kathryn Lasky's *Dear America: Dreams in the Golden Country, The Diary of Zipporah Feldman, a Jewish Immigrant Girl* (New York: Scholastic Inc., 1998) includes details of immigrant life around the turn of the century, as does Raymond Bial's *Tenement: Immigrant Life on the Lower East Side* (Boston: Houghton Mifflin Company, 2002).

The Kheel Center at Cornell University (http:// www.ilr.cornell.edu/ trianglefire) features an Internet exhibit on the Triangle factory fire.

The Lower East Side Tenement Museum in New York City (www.tenement.org) has a number of tenement tours available as well as a sweatshop exhibit.

Other resources on the shirtwaist strike and Triangle factory fire include John McClymer's *The Triangle Strike and Fire* (Fort Worth, Tex.: Harcourt Brace College Publishers, 1998) and Leon Stein's *Out of the Sweatshop: The Struggle for Industrial Democracy* (New York: Quadrangle/The New York Times Book Co., 1977). Rose Cohen's memoir, *Out of the Shadow,* has been reprinted in paperback (Ithaca, N.Y.: Cornell University Press, 1995).

ACKNOWLEDGMENTS

Many people helped make this book possible. I owe a tremendous debt of gratitude to Amy Griffin and Lisa Sandell for their perceptive editing and support. Dr. Donna R. Gabaccia, Charles H. Stone Professor of American History at the University of North Carolina at Charlotte, was generous in answering questions related to Italian immigrants. Steve Long, curator, the Lower East Side Tenement Museum, and Jennifer Guglielmo, assistant professor of history at Smith College, gave of their time to read the manuscript and make suggestions.

I would also like to thank staff members at libraries and museums who assisted with research and photographs. Special thanks to Michael Dempsey at Cornell University Press; Barbara Morley and Patrizia Sione at Cornell University's Kheel Center for Labor-Management Documentation and Archives; Eleanor Gillers at the New-York Historical Society; Anne Guernsey at The Museum of the City of New

York; Kerry McLaughlin at The Historical Society of Pennsylvania for her efforts in finding a photograph of Leonard Covello; Janice Madhu at George Eastman House; as well as the staff of the New York Public Library, the University of California at Riverside/California Museum of Photography, the Library of Congress, and New York University.

Special thanks to Michele Hill for her help with photography research and selection and her devoted friendship. I thank my husband, Andy Thomas, and children, Rebekah and Dimitri, for their patience and support, and their efforts to keep the cat off my lap and the turtle off my feet during the writing of this book. I am grateful to Elisa Johnston and her mother, the late Laurie Johnston, for the generous use of Elisa's childhood home on Jones Street in Greenwich Village. I appreciate the support of my agent, Steven Malk, as well as my colleagues at Whitman College, especially Barbara Noseworthy, for my "other" career. A special thanks to Susan Campbell Bartoletti for her advice, and for the encouragement and friendship of Deborah Wiles and Jane Kurtz. Any errors are solely my own.

SELECTED BIBLIOGRAPHY

ANTIN, MARY. *The Promised Land.* Boston: Houghton Mifflin Company, 1969. First published by *The Atlantic Monthly,* 1911 and 1912.

BALES, CAROL. *Tales of the Elders: A Memory Book of Men and Women Who Came to America as Immigrants, 1900–1930.* Chicago: Follett Publishing Company, 1977.

BARTOLETTI, SUSAN CAMPBELL. *Black Potatoes: The Story of the Great Irish Famine, 1845–1850.* Boston: Houghton Mifflin Company, 2001.

BINDER, FREDERICK M., and DAVID M. REIMERS. *All the Nations under Heaven: An Ethnic and Racial History of New York City.* New York: Columbia University Press, 1995.

BREMNER, ROBERT H. "The Big Flat: History of a New York Tenement House." *The American Historical Review,* Volume 54, Issue 1, October 1958, pp. 54–62.

CANTOR, EDDIE. *My Life Is in Your Hands.* New York: Blue Ribbon Books, Inc., 1932.

CHAPIN, ROBERT COIT. *The Standard of Living Among Workingmen's Families in New York City.* New York: Charities Publication Committee, Russell Sage Foundation, 1909.

CHOTZINOFF, SAMUEL. *A Lost Paradise: Early Reminiscences.* New York: Alfred A. Knopf, 1955.

COHEN, MIRIAM. *Workshop to Office: Two Generations of Italian Women in New York City, 1900–1950.* Ithaca, N.Y.: Cornell University Press, 1992.

COHEN, MORRIS RAPHAEL. *A Dreamer's Journey.* Boston: The Beacon Press, 1949.

COHEN, ROSE. *Out of the Shadow: A Russian Jewish Girlhood on the Lower East Side.* Ithaca, N.Y.: Cornell University Press, 1995. Originally published 1918.

COVELLO, LEONARD, with GUIDO D'AGOSTINO. *The Heart Is the Teacher.* New York: McGraw-Hill Book Company, Inc., 1958.

DAY, JARED N. *Urban Castles: Tenement Housing and Landlord Activism in New York City, 1890–1943.* New York: Columbia University Press, 1999.

DEFOREST, ROBERT W., and LAWRENCE VEILLER, ed. *The Tenement House Problem, Including the Report of the New York State Tenement House Commission of 1900.* New York: The MacMillan Company, 1903.

ETS, MARIE HALL. *Rosa: The Life of an Italian Immigrant.* Madison: University of Wisconsin Press, 1970.

EWEN, ELIZABETH. *Immigrant Women in the Land of Dollars: Life and Culture on the Lower East Side, 1890–1925.* New York: Monthly Review Press, 1985.

FELT, JEREMY P. *Hostages of Fortune: Child Labor Reform in New York State.* Syracuse: Syracuse University Press, 1965.

FRIEDMAN-KASABA, KATHIE. *Memories of Migration: Gender, Ethnicity and Work in the Lives of Jewish and Italian Women in New York, 1870–1924.* Albany: State University of New York Press, 1996.

FROWNE, SADIE. "The Story of a Sweatshop Girl." *The Independent* 54 (September 25, 1902), pp. 2279–82.

GABACCIA, DONNA R. *From Sicily to Elizabeth Street: Housing and Social Change among Italian Immigrants, 1880–1930.* Albany: State University of New York Press, 1984.

GOODMAN, CARY. *Choosing Sides: Playground and Street Life on the Lower East Side.* New York: Schocken Books, 1979.

HINDUS, MAURICE. *Green Worlds: An Informal Chronicle.* New York: Doubleday, Foran & Company, Inc., 1938.

———. *A Traveler in Two Worlds.* Introduction by Milton Hindus. Garden City, N.Y.: Doubleday & Company, Inc., 1971.

HOWE, IRVING, and KENNETH LIBO. *How We Lived: A Documentary History of Immigrant Jews in America.* New York: Richard Marek Publishers, 1979.

HOWE, IRVING. *World of Our Fathers: The Journey of the East European Jews to America and the Life They Found and Made.* New York: Harcourt Brace Jovanovich, 1976.

KAMMEN, MICHAEL. *Colonial New York: A History.* New York: Charles Scribner's Sons, 1975.

KESSNER, THOMAS. *The Golden Door: Italian and Jewish Immigrant Mobility in New York City, 1880–1915.* New York: Oxford University Press, 1977.

KISSELOFF, JEFF. *You Must Remember This: An Oral History of Manhattan from the 1800s to World War II.* San Diego: Harcourt Brace Jovanovich, 1989.

LA SORTE, MICHAEL. *La Merica: Images of Italian Greenhorn Experience.* Philadelphia: Temple University Press, 1985.

LOWER EAST SIDE TENEMENT MUSEUM. *A Tenement Story: The History of 97 Orchard Street and the Lower East Side Tenement Museum.* New York: Lower East Side Tenement Museum, 1999.

MAFFI, MARIO. *Gateway to the Promised Land: Ethnic Cultures in New York's Lower East Side.* New York: New York University Press, 1995.

MCCLYMER, JOHN F. *The Triangle Strike and Fire.* Fort Worth: Harcourt Brace College Publishers, 1998.

MENDELSOHN, JOYCE. *The Lower East Side Remembered and Revisited.* New York: The Lower East Side Press, 2001.

MORE, LOUISE BOLARD. *Wage-Earners' Budgets: A Study of Standards and Cost of Living in New York City.* New York: Henry Holt and Company, 1907. Reprinted, New York: Arno Press and the *New York Times,* 1971.

ODENCRANTZ, LOUISE C. *Italian Women in Industry: A Study of Conditions in New York City.* New York: Russell Sage Foundation, 1919.

PANUNZIO, CONSTANTINE. *The Soul of an Immigrant.* New York: The Macmillan Company, 1922.

PEEBLES, ROBERT W. *Leonard Covello: A Study of an Immigrant's Contribution to New York City.* New York: Arno Press, 1978.

RAVAGE, M. E. *An American in the Making: The Life Story of an Immigrant.* New York: Harper & Brothers Publishers, 1917.

RIIS, JACOB. *How the Other Half Lives: Studies among the Tenements of New York.* New York: Penguin Books, 1997. First published by Charles Scribner's Sons, 1890.

RUSKAY, SOPHIE. *Horsecars and Cobblestones.* New York: The Beechhurst Press, 1948.

SAFRAN, ROSEY. "The Washington Place Fire." *The Independent* 70. (April 20, 1911) pp. 840–41.

SALZ, EVELYN, ed. *Selected Letters of Mary Antin.* Syracuse, N.Y.: Syracuse University Press, 2000.

SCHOFIELD, ANN. *To Do and to Be: Portraits of Four Women Activists, 1893–1986.* Boston: Northeastern University Press, 1997.

STEIN, LEON. *The Triangle Fire.* New York: Lippincott, 1962.

STEIN, LEON, ed. *Out of the Sweatshop: The Struggle for Industrial Democracy.* New York: Quadrangle/The *New York Times* Book Co., 1977.

VAN KLEECK, MARY. *Artificial Flower Makers.* New York: Survey Associates, Inc., Russell Sage Foundation, 1913.

———. *Working Girls in Evening Schools: A Statistical Study.* New York: Survey Associates, Inc., Russell Sage Foundation, 1914.

VEILLER, LAWRENCE. *A Model Tenement House Law.* New York: Charities Publication Committee, Russell Sage Foundation, 1910.

NEWSPAPERS, MICROFILM, ORAL HISTORIES

INS History, Genealogy & Education Website: http://www.ins.usdoj.gov.

Institute of Labor and Industrial Relations (University of Michigan–Wayne State University), Women and Work Program. The Twentieth Century Trade Union Woman — Vehicle for Social Change. Oral History Project, Part I, No. 23. *Pauline Newman. International Ladies' Garment Workers' Union.* November 1976. Interview by Barbara Wertheimer.

The New York Call; The New York Times; The New York Herald Tribune.

Triangle Fire Trial Transcript. Cornell University, Kheel Center, School of Industrial and Labor Relations.

TEXT PERMISSIONS

WE GRATEFULLY ACKNOWLEDGE PERMISSION TO QUOTE FROM THE FOLLOWING SOURCES: Excerpts from *A Dreamer's Journey* by Morris Raphael Cohen, Boston: The Beacon Press, 1949, used by permission of Beacon Press. Excerpts from *A Lost Paradise* by Samuel Chotzinoff, copyright © 1953, 1955 by Samuel Chotzinoff, used by permission of Alfred A. Knopf, a division of Random House, Inc. Excerpts from *An American in the Making* by M.E. Ravage, New York and London: Harper & Brothers Publishers, 1936, used by permission of HarperCollins Publishers, Inc. Excerpts from *Green Worlds* by Maurice Hindus, New York: Doubleday, Doran & Company, Inc., 1938; and *A Traveler in Two Worlds* by Maurice Hindus, introduction by Milton Hindus, Garden City, New York: Doubleday and Company, 1971, used by permission of Francis McLernan Hindus. Excerpts from *The Heart Is the Teacher* by Leonard Covello with Guido D'Agostino, New York: McGraw-Hill Book Company, Inc., 1958, used by permission of Blassingame, McCauley and Wood. Excerpts from *How We Lived: A Documentary History of Immigrant Jews in America* by Irving Howe and Kenneth Libo, New York: Richard Marek Publishers, 1979, used by permission of Richard Marek Publishers, Inc. Excerpt from *Immigrant Women in the Land of Dollars: Life and Culture on the Lower East Side, 1890-1925* by Elizabeth Ewen, copyright © 1985 by Monthly Review Press, reprinted by permission of Monthly Review Foundation. Excerpts from *Letter to Michael and Hugh from P. M. Newman*, May 1951, ILGWU Archives, Kheel Center for Labor Management Documentation and Archives, Cornell University, Ithaca, NY, used by permission of the Kheel Center for Labor Management Documentation and Archives, Cornell University, from "The Triangle Factory Fire," http://www.ilr.cornell.edu/trianglefire/texts/letters/newman_letter.html. Excerpts from *My Life Is in Your Hands* by Eddie Cantor, New York: Harper & Brothers Publishers, 1928, used by permission of HarperCollins Publishers, Inc. Excerpts from interview with Pauline Newman used by permission of the Institute of Labor and Industrial Relations, Women and Work Program, University of Michigan-Wayne State University and The Bentley Library, University of Michigan (this interview was part of the *New York Times Oral History Program, The Twentieth Century Trade Union Woman: Vehicle for Social Change Oral History Project, Part 1, No. 23 Pauline Newman, International Ladies' Garment Workers' Union*, interview by Barbara Wertheimer, 1978). Excerpts from *Out of the Shadow: A Russian Jewish Girlhood on the Lower East Side* by Rose Cohen, introduction by Thomas Dublin, Ithaca: Cornell University Press, 1995, used by permission of Cornell University Press. Excerpts from *Rosa: The Life of an Italian Immigrant* by Marie Hall Ets, University of Wisconsin Press, 1970, used by permission of University of Wisconsin Press. Excerpts from *The Soul of an Immigrant* by Constantine Panunzio, New York: The Macmillan Company, 1922, used by permission of Mrs. Constantine Panunzio. Excerpts from *Tales of the Elders: A Memory Book of Men and Women Who Came to America as Immigrants, 1900-1930* by Carol Bales, Chicago: Follett Publishing Company, 1977, used by permission of Carol Bales. Excerpts from *You Must Remember This: An Oral History of Manhattan from the 1890s to World War II*, copyright © 1989 by Jeff Kisseloff, reprinted by permission of Harcourt Inc.

NOTES

FOREWORD

Immigrants: Kessner, Thomas, *The Golden Door: Italian and Jewish Immigrant Mobility in New York City 1880–1915*. New York: Oxford University Press, 1977, p. 5.

Binder, Frederick M. and Reimers, David M., *All the Nations under Heaven: An Ethnic and Racial History of New York City*. New York: Columbia University Press, 1995, pp. 102–105.

COMING TO THE GOLDEN LAND

"The gold you will find . . .": Covello, Leonard, with D'Agostino, Guido, *The Heart Is the Teacher*. New York: McGraw-Hill Book Company, Inc., 1958, p. 18.

Avigliano and letter-writing: Ibid., pp. 14–16.

"You must watch": Ibid., p. 4.

catching butterflies: Ibid.

"Some people said . . .": Bales, Carol, *Tales of the Elders: A Memory Book of Men and Women Who Came to America as Immigrants, 1900–1930*. Chicago: Follett Publishing Company, 1977, p. 17.

yards of calico, rye: Hindus, Maurice, *Green Worlds: An Informal Chronicle*. New York: Doubleday, Foran & Company, Inc., 1938, p. 80.

soap: Ibid., p. 75.

stories of New York: Ravage, M. E., *An American in the Making*. New York: Harper & Brothers Publishers, 1917, 1936, pp. 11–21.

economic conditions: Kessner, *The Golden Door*, p. 15.

shtetl: Howe, Irving, *World of Our Fathers: The Journey of the East European Jews to America and the Life They Found and Made*. New York and London: Harcourt Brace Jovanovich, 1976, p. 10.

housework: Cohen, Morris Raphael, *A Dreamer's Journey*. Boston and Illinois: The Beacon Press and The Free Press, 1949, pp. 17–18.

pogroms and economic situation: Rischin, Moses, *The Promised City: New York's Jews 1870–1914*. New York: Harper Torchbooks, 1962, pp. 24–26.

"I was only . . .": Bales, *Tales of the Elders*, p. 16.

"So at last . . .": Antin, Mary, *The Promised Land*. Boston: Houghton Mifflin Company, 1969. First published by the *Atlantic Monthly*, 1911 and 1912, p. 162.

Mamma Clementine and Covello family: Peebles, Robert W., *Leonard Covello: A Study of an Immigrant's Contribution to New York City*. New York: Arno Press, 1978, pp. 40–50.

saying goodbye: Covello, *The Heart Is the Teacher*, pp. 17–18.

leaving for America: Ravage, *An American in the Making*, p. 51.

"I understand it now . . .": Ibid., p. 55.

family departure: Hindus, *Green Worlds*, p. 77.

"In the morning . . .": Antin, *The Promised Land*, p. 167.

"the station . . .": Ibid., p. 169.

"My heart leaped . . .": Ravage, *An American in the Making*, p. 55.

"home was something . . .": Hindus, *Green Worlds*, p. 83.

"On the fourth day . . .": Ets, Marie Hall, *Rosa: The Life of an Italian Immigrant*. Madison: University of Wisconsin Press, 1970, p. 163.

"It was horrible . . .": Institute of Labor and Industrial Relations (University of Michigan – Wayne State University), Women and Work Program. *The Twentieth Century Trade Union Woman: Vehicle for Social Change, Oral History Project, Part I, No. 23, Pauline Newman, International Ladies' Garment Workers' Union*, November 1976, Interview by Barbara Wertheimer, p. 2.

"Another time . . .": Ibid.

"Then one day . . .": Ets, *Rosa*, pp. 164–165.

"Once during . . .": Covello, *The Heart Is the Teacher*, p. 20.

reuniting with father: Cohen, Rose, *Out of the Shadow: A Russian Jewish Girlhood on the Lower East Side*. Ithaca, N.Y.: Cornell University Press, 1995. Originally published 1918, pp. 64–65.

Native Americans: Kammen, Michael, *Colonial New York: A History*. New York: Charles Scribner's Sons, 1975, p. 10.

hilly island: Mendelsohn, Joyce. *The Lower East Side Remembered & Revisited*. New York: The Lower East Side Press, 2001, p. 2.

size of city: Day, Jared, *Urban Castles: Tenement Housing and Landlord Activism*. New York: Columbia University Press, 1999, p. 11.

population and slavery abolished: Mendelsohn, *The Lower East Side Remembered & Revisited*, p. 4.

TENEMENTS: SHUTTING OUT THE SKY

"I shall never forget . . .": Ravage, *An American in the Making*, pp. 66–67.

ferryboat ride from Ellis Island: Covello, *The Heart Is the Teacher*, p. 20.

"The cobbled streets . . .": Ibid., p. 21.

warm sunlight: Ibid.

"My thoughts . . .": Cohen, *Out of the Shadow*, p. 69.

"You couldn't get to love . . .": Hindus, Maurice, *A Traveler in Two Worlds*. Garden City, New York: Doubleday & Company, Inc., 1971, p. 115.

Chinese immigration: Binder and Reimers, *All the Nations under Heaven*, p. 108; correspondence from Jennifer Guglielmo, January 27, 2003.

Little Africa: Mendelsohn, *The Lower East Side Remembered & Revisited*, p. 5.

blacks: Binder and Reimers, *All the Nations under Heaven*, p. 109.

studies: correspondence from Jennifer Guglielmo, January 27, 2003.

Jews/Lower East Side: Mendelsohn, *The Lower East Side Remembered & Revisited*, pp. 6–9; Binder and Reimers, *All the Nations under Heaven*, pp. 114–115.

people per acre: Howe, *World of Our Fathers*, p. 69.

tenements: DeForest, Robert W., and Veiller, Lawrence, ed., *The Tenement House Problem, Including the Report of the New York State Tenement House Commission of 1900*. New York: The MacMillan Company, 1903, p. 37.

"In the stifling July . . .": Riis, Jacob, *How the Other Half Lives: Studies Among the Tenements of New York*. New York: Penguin Books, 1997. First published by Charles Scribner's Sons, 1890, p. 125.

Big Flat: Bremner, Robert H., "The Big Flat, History of a New York Tenement House," *The American Historical Review*, Volume 64, Issue I (October 1958), pp. 54–62.

"a tenement without facilities . . .": Newman, *Oral History Project*, p. 33.

tenements: Day, *Urban Castles*, p. 16, quoting Philip Hone, *The Diary of Philip Hone*. New York: Dodd, Mead, 1927, pp. 245–246.

early reform efforts: Ibid., pp. 24–29.

"It is said . . .": Riis, *How the Other Half Lives*, p. 82.

"Suppose we look . . .": Ibid., p. 37.

"The rays of the sun . . .": Ibid., p. 35.

"strip of smoke-colored sky": Ibid., p. 38.

"What are you going to do . . .": Ibid., p. 6.

three cheers: Riis, *How the Other Half Lives*, introduction by Luc Sante, p. xxi.

eliminating dark inner courts: Day, *Urban Castles*, p. 69.

"you weren't bothered . . .": Ibid.

rent strikes: Newman, *Oral History Project*, p.4; Day, *Urban Castles*, p. 75.

rear tenements: More, Louise Bolard, *Wage-Earners' Budgets: A Study of Standards and Cost of Living in New York City*. New York: Henry Holt and Company, 1907. Reprinted, New York: Arno Press & The New York Times, 1971, p. 131.

"the families did not have . . .": Odencrantz, Louise, *Italian Women in Industry: A Study of Conditions in New York City*. New York: Russell Sage Foundation, 1919, p. 14.

new-law tenements: Ibid., p. 132.

home decorations: Ibid., p. 138.

"Courage! . . .": Covello, *The Heart Is the Teacher*, p. 22.

"I saw many streets . . .": Cohen, *Out of the Shadow*, p. 76.

SETTLING IN: BOARDERS AND GREENHORNS

"Life here . . .": Cohen, *Out of the Shadow*, p. 73.

"rich enough . . .": Ravage, *An American in the Making*, p. 70.

"crumpled bit…": Ibid., p. 62.

"puffing of steam engines . . .": Ibid., p. 72

"We had to keep . . .": Kisseloff, Jeff, *You Must Remember This: An Oral History of Manhattan from the 1800s to World War II*. San Diego: Harcourt Brace Jovanovich, 1989, p. 19.

partner households: Gabaccia, Donna R., *From Sicily to Elizabeth Street: Housing and Social Change among Italian Immigrants, 1880–1930*. Albany: State University of New York Press, 1984, p. 75.

one out of every four: Ewen, Elizabeth, *Immigrant Women in the Land of Dollars: Life and Culture on the Lower East Side 1890–1925*. New York: Monthly Review Press, 1985, p. 119.

"We liked moving . . .": Cohen, *Out of the Shadow*, p. 186.

"This my grandmother . . .": Cantor, Eddie, *My Life Is in Your Hands*. New York: Blue Ribbon Books, Inc., 1932, pp. 16–17.

"someone dear from home . . .": Cohen, *Out of the Shadow*, p. 77.

"The sky is the same . . .": Ibid.

"the only way . . .": Ravage, *An American in the Making*, pp. 93–94.

"I was such a greenhorn . . .": Ewen, *Immigrant Women in the Land of Dollars*, p. 68.

"Our initiation . . .": Antin, *The Promised Land*, p. 135.

"Shoes . . .": Cohen, *Out of the Shadow*, p. 151.

"Fetchke . . .": Antin, *The Promised Land*, pp. 187–188.

"It did not seem to matter . . .": Ravage, *An American in the Making*, p. 78.

name changes: Smith, Marian L., "American Names/Declaring Independence," INS History, Genealogy & Education, http://www.ins.usdoj.gov/graphics/aboutins/history/articles/NameEssay.html, accessed 12/8/02.

"What happened . . .": Covello, *The Heart Is the Teacher*, pp. 29–31.

EVERYONE WORKED ON

"Father, does everybody . . .": Cohen, *Out of the Shadow*, p. 74.

"Everybody hustled . . .": Ravage, *An American in the Making*, p. 94.

"peddlers . . .": Ibid., pp. 95–96.

"How is business . . .": Ibid., pp. 97–98.

"Father used to buy . . .": Cohen, *Out of the Shadow*, p. 83.

"When as usual . . .": Ibid., p. 108.

"a fuzzy brown coat . . .": Ibid., p. 168.

first morning of work: Ibid., p. 108.

"My hands trembled . . .": Ibid., p. 110.

"Seven o'clock came . . .": Ibid., p. 111.

"I hurried . . .": Ibid., pp. 112–113.

"I could not realize . . .": Ibid., p. 139.

"the faster you work...": McClymer, John, *The Triangle Strike and Fire*, Fort Worth: Harcourt Brace College Publishers, 1998, p. 15.

"Oh how I'll scrub,": Cohen, *Out of the Shadow*, p. 142.

"Mamma . . .": Ibid., p. 149.

"When the children . . .": Ibid., p. 160.

"wrapped in . . .": Ibid., p. 170.

every hour: Ibid., p. 181.

"In Italy . . .": Odencrantz, *Italian Women in Industry*, p. 176.

"While exact figures . . .": Felt, Jeremy P., *Hostages of Fortune: Child Labor Reform in New York State*. Syracuse N.Y.: Syracuse University Press, 1965, p. 1.

Education Law: Ibid., p. 7.

"In 1896 . . .": Ibid., p. 25.

factory legislation: Ibid., pp. 26–37.

1902 legislation: Ibid., pp. 38–56.

"By 1900 . . .": Ibid., p. 63.

national legislation: Ibid., pp. 215–224.

hand-dipping chocolates: Odencrantz, *Italian Women in Industry*, pp. 139–140.

occupations: Chapin, Robert Coit, *The Standard of Living among Workingmen's Families in New York City*. New York: Charities Publication Committee, Russell Sage Foundation, 1909, pp. 44–56.

"I practiced . . .": Panunzio, Constantine, *The Soul of an Immigrant*. New York: The Macmillan Company, 1922, pp. 76–77.

home workers: Van Kleeck, Mary, *Artificial Flower Makers*. New York: Survey Associates, Inc., Russell Sage Foundation, 1913, pp. 100–101.

artificial-flower makers: Ibid., pp. 94–95.

"Fourteen hours . . .": Cohen, *Out of the Shadow*, p. 125.

"You were watched . . .": Newman, *Oral History Project*, p. 17.

"If you don't come in . . .": Ibid., p. 15.

"Every day . . .": Newman, Pauline. Letter to Michael and Hugh Owens, typescript, May 1954, International Ladies' Garment Workers' Union Archives, Cornell University, Kheel Center for Labor-Management Documentation and Archives, p. 20.

"In a small way . . .": Ibid.

"Of all the . . .": *The New York Call*, January 3, 1910.

"I have listened . . .": Stein, Leon, ed., *Out of the Sweatshop: The Struggle for Industrial Democracy*. New York: Quadrangle/The New York Times Book Co., Inc., p. 70.

"The door was locked . . .": Safran, Rosey, "The Washington Place Fire." *The Independent*, No. 70 (April 20, 1911), pp. 840–841.

"the flames were already . . .": Ibid.

"The whole door . . .": McClymer, *The Triangle Strike*, p. 116.

memorial meeting: Ibid., p. 101.

"It seemed . . .": Newman, *Oral History Project*, p. 32.

ON THE STREETS: PUSHCARTS, PICKLES, AND PLAY

"I loved . . .": Hindus, *A Traveler in Two Worlds*, p. 43.

"I contented myself . . .": Ibid., pp. 41–42.

"a solemn duff . . .": Ibid., p. 43.

"works of art . . .": Ibid., pp. 42–43.

Hester Street: Ibid., p. 44.

"Orchard and Ludlow . . .": Kisseloff, *You Must Remember This*, p.19.

"We would play . . .": Chotzinoff, Samuel, *A Lost Paradise: Early Reminiscences*. New York: Alfred A. Knopf, 1955, p. 71.

street play: Goodman, Cary, *Choosing Sides: Playground and Street Life on the Lower East Side*. New York: Schocken Books, 1979, p. 16.

horse in gutter: Chotzinoff, *A Lost Paradise*, p. 62.

"We had about ten horses . . .": Kisseloff, *You Must Remember This*, pp. 29–30.

"Cheese it! . . .": Chotzinoff, *A Lost Paradise*, p. 84.

"Following the fire engines . . .": Ibid., p. 89.

playing tag: Ibid., p. 90.

Italian neighborhoods: Gabaccia, *From Sicily to Elizabeth Street*, p. 97.

Italian women: Ewen, *Immigrant Women in the Land of Dollars*, p. 166; correspondence with Jennifer Guglielmo, January 27, 2003.

"the true heart . . .": Maffi, Mario, *Gateway to the Promised Land: Ethnic Cultures in New York's Lower East Side*. New York: New York University Press, 1995, p. 75.

soapbox: Newman, *Oral History Project*, p. 13.

"[The streets] . . .": Hindus, *A Traveler in Two Worlds*, p. 46.

"The play . . .": Chotzinoff, *A Lost Paradise*, p. 97.

"Each street . . .": Cantor, *My Life Is in Your Hands*, p. 27.

"We bought ours . . .": Kisseloff, *You Must Remember This*, p. 43.

"I got so . . .": Cantor, *My Life Is in Your Hands*, p. 21.

"At first . . .": Ruskay, Sophie, *Horsecars and Cobblestones*. New York: The Beechhurst Press, 1948, p. 50.

"My father . . .": Kisseloff, *You Must Remember This*, pp. 31–32.

sugar: Hindus, *Green Worlds*, p. 90.

"sweet rolls . . .": Ibid.

Friday nights: Chotzinoff, *A Lost Paradise*, pp. 73–74.

"corned beefs . . .": Ibid., pp. 188–89.

"In Avigliano . . .": Covello, *The Heart Is the Teacher*, p. 36.

"meat soup . . .": Howe, Irving, and Libo, Kenneth, *How We Lived: A Documentary History of Immigrant Jews in America*. New York: Richard Marek Publishers, 1979, p. 44.

family budgets: More, *Wage-Earners' Budgets*, pp. 217–218.

A NEW LANGUAGE, A NEW LIFE

"We had to visit . . .": Antin, *The Promised Land*, p. 187.

Romanian restaurant: Ravage, *An American in the Making*, p. 100.

Educational Alliance: Howe, *World of Our Fathers*, pp. 230–233.

"You have to consider . . .": Kisseloff, *You Must Remember This*, p. 81.

"I cannot tell you . . .": Ravage, *An American in the Making*, p. 177.

"Goota boy . . .": Hindus, *Green Worlds*, pp. 95–96.

"In less than a week . . .": Ibid., p. 95.

"Every day . . .": Hindus, *A Traveler in Two Worlds*, p. 45.

"My head swam . . .": Hindus, *Green Worlds*, p. 110; Hindus, *A Traveler in Two Worlds*, p. 53.

"grope along . . .": Covello, *The Heart Is the Teacher*, p. 38.

"It was rush, rush . . .": Ibid.

"In me you see . . .": Ibid., p. 41.

"I don't like the work . . .": Van Kleeck, Mary, *Working Girls in Evening Schools: A Statistical Study*. New York: Survey Associates, Inc., Russell Sage Foundation, 1914, p. 142.

working papers: Ewen, *Immigrant Women in the Land of Dollars*, p. 193.

night classes: Van Kleeck, *Working Girls in*

Evening Schools, p. 14.

"Going to night school . . .": Newman, *Oral History Project*, p. 6.

"And every night . . .": Ibid.

"A child . . .": Cohen, *Out of the Shadow*, p. 246.

"After working all day...": Bales, *Tales of the Elders*, pp. 19–20.

"We soon got the idea . . .": Covello, *The Heart Is the Teacher*, p. 43.

keeping mothers away from school: Ibid., p. 47.

"How could parents . . .": Ibid., pp. 47–48.

"If I could read . . .": Cohen, *Out of the Shadow*, p. 252.

"There is hardly . . .": Ibid., p. 50.

"You're just as good . . .": Ibid., p. 51.

LOOKING TO THE FUTURE: WILL IT EVER BE DIFFERENT?

"I knew . . .": Hindus, *Green Worlds*, p. 106.

"College costs money . . .": Covello, *The Heart Is the Teacher*, p. 61.

marriage decision: Cohen, *Out of the Shadow*, pp. 205–206.

"the monotonous . . .": Covello, *The Heart Is the Teacher*, p. 64.

"golden dreams . . .": Ibid., p. 18.

"Is it too late . . .": Ibid., p. 62.

"Narduccio, my son . . .": Ibid., p. 65.

"My pupils . . .": Ibid., p. 215

death: "Leonard Covello, 94, Ex-Head of East Harlem School," *The New York Times*, August 20, 1982, p. 4.

Rose Cohen: Cohen, *Out of the Shadow*, introduction by Thomas Dublin, pp. ix–xix.

Maurice Hindus: Hindus, *A Traveler in Two Worlds*, introduction by Milton Hindus, pp. 13–15.

Pauline Newman: "Pauline Newman, an Early Organizer of Clothing Workers," *The New York Times*, April 10, 1986, p. 26.; Schofield, Ann, *To Do and to Be: Portraits of Four Women Activists, 1893–1986*. Boston: Northeastern University Press, 1997, pp. 82–112.

Marcus Ravage: *Book Review Digest*, 2002; Ravage, *An American in the Making*, p. xvii.

improving conditions: Kessner, *The Golden Door*, pp. 167–169.

staying in school: Cohen, Miriam, *From Workshop to Office: Two Generations of Italian Women in New York City, 1900-1950*. Ithaca: Cornell University Press, 1992, pp. 158–159.

"the echoes from . . .": Cohen, *A Dreamer's Journey*, p. xiii.

PHOTO CREDITS

Grateful acknowledgment is made for permission to reprint the following: FRONT COVER: Collection of the New-York Historical Society, Negative no. 37357; BACK COVER: Museum of the City of New York, Byron Collection, No. 93.1.1.15380; TITLE PAGE: Museum of the City of New York, Jacob A. Riis Collection, #502, No. 90.13.3.125; FOREWORD: New-York Historical Society, Negative no. 37382; VOICES IN THIS BOOK: Rose Cohen: Cornell University Press; Leonard Covello: The Balch Institute Collections, The Historical Society of Pennsylvania, detail from Leonard Covello [PG 107/354]; Maurice Hindus: Colgate University Archives; Pauline Newman: UNITE Archives Kheel Center, Cornell University, Ithaca, New York, No. 14853-3901; Marcus Eli Ravage: Courtesy Ravage/Clausen Family; Page xii: Keystone-Mast Collection, UCR/California Museum of Photography, University of California, Riverside, No. KU72962; Page 3: Library of Congress; Page 5: From *The Promised Land*, by Mary Antin, Houghton Mifflin; Page 10: Library of Congress, Reproduction no. LC-USZC2-2509; Page 11: Keystone-Mast Collection, UCR/California Museum of Photography, University of California, Riverside, No. X288; Page 12: New York Public Library, Photo by Lewis Hine; Page 13: National Archives of Public Health Service, No. 90-G-125-29; Page 16: Museum of the City of New York, Byron Collection, No. 93.1.1.15380; Page 18: New-York Historical Society, Alexander Alland Collection, No. 2357, Negative no. 71879; Page 19: Museum of the City of New York, Jacob A. Riis Collection, #502, No. 90.13.3.125; Page 20: Map by Mike Regan; Page 21: Museum of the City of New York, Gift of Tenement House Department, N.Y.C., No. 31.93.11; Page 23: New York Public Library, Photo by Lewis Hine; Page 24: New York Public Library; Page 25: Library of Congress, Reproduction no. LC-USZ62-113814; Page 26: New-York Historical Society, Negative no. 33547; Page 29: Museum of the City of New York, Jacob A. Riis Collection, #75, No. 90.13.1.79; Page 32: New York Public Library, Photo by Lewis Hine; Page 34: Museum of the City of New York, Byron Collection, No. 93.1.1.17888; Page 35: Museum of the City of New York, Gift of Tenement House Department, N.Y.C., No. 31.93.14; Page 36: New-York Historical Society, Armbruster Collection, Negative no. 71078; Page 39: New York Public Library, Photo by Lewis Hine; Page 40: Library of Congress, Reproduction no. LC-D4-36490; Page 42: New-York Historical Society, Negative no. 76527; Page 46: New York Public Library, Photo by Lewis Hine, Unit 2, No. 77; Page 48: New York Public Library, Photo by Lewis Hine, Unit 2, No. 41; Page 51: New York Public Library, Hine Collection, Unit 3, No. 32; Page 52: Museum of the City of New York, Jacob A. Riis Collection, #1, No. 90.13.1.50; Page 54: New York Public Library, Photo by Lewis Hine, Unit 2, No. 81; Page 56: New York Public Library, Photo by Lewis Hine, No. 91PH056.015; Page 60: New York Public Library, Photo by Lewis Hine, Unit 2, No. 46; Page 64: Library of Congress, Reproduction no. LC-USZ62-49516; Page 67: Library of Congress, Reproduction no. LC-USZ62-34984; Page 68: UNITE Archives Kheel Center, Cornell University, Ithaca, New York, No. 14853-3901; Page 69: UNITE Archives Kheel Center, Cornell University, Ithaca, New York, No. 14853-3901; Page 70: New York Public Library, Photo by Lewis Hine, Unit 2, No. 80; Page 72: Museum of the City of New York, Byron Collection, No. 93.1.1.18129; Page 73: Library of Congress, George Grantham Bain Collection, Reproduction no. LC-USZ62-119372; Page 74: Library of Congress, Reproduction no. LC-D401-13645; Page 75: New York Public Library, Photo by Lewis Hine; Page 76: New York Public Library, Photo by Lewis Hine, No. 91 PH056.122; Page 79: New-York Historical Society, Armbruster Collection, No. 86, Negative no. 43269; Page 80: Library of Congress, Photo by Jacob A. Riis, Reproduction no. LC-USZ62-72472; Page 81: New-York Historical Society, Photo by Frank M. Ingalls, Negative no. 624200-426; Page 82: Library of Congress, Reproduction no. LC-D401-13585; Page 85: New-York Historical Society, Negative no. 37277; Page 86: New York Public Library, Photo by Lewis Hine; Page 89: New-York Historical Society, Negative no. 71962; Page 90: Museum of the City of New York, Jacob A. Riis Collection, #CC, No. 90.13.1.40; Page 92: Museum of the City of New York, Jacob A. Riis Collection, #253, No. 90.13.1.257; Page 94: Museum of the City of New York, Jacob A. Riis Collection, #170, No. 90.13.1.173; Page 97: New-York Historical Society, Negative no. 75547; Page 98: New-York Historical Society, Negative no. 75546; Page 100: New York Public Library; AFTERWORD: George Eastman House, Photo by Barbara Puorro Galasso.

INDEX